Conversation Skills

Secrets for Introverts on How to Analyze People, Handle Small Talk with Confidence, Overcome Social Anxiety and Highly Effective Communication Tips for Networking with People

Contents

Introduction

The following chapters will discuss why communication matters, conversation fundamentals, connecting with people and social survival.

Let me introduce you to four people who will be your case studies throughout this book: Rebecca, Larry, Chris and Kelly.

- Rebecca is an introvert who is finding it challenging to contribute to discussions at work. Rebecca's goal is to share her ideas with her team– and be heard!
- Larry is an introvert, but he has adapted well in an extrovert's world at work. Larry's goal is to improve his networking skills through better conversation skills.
- Chris is an introvert, tends to be anxious and, embarrassingly for her, has been called terribly shy. Chris' goal is to be less stressed at work.

- Kelly is not an introvert, but still wants to improve his conversation skills. Kelly's goal is to understand what makes his introvert friends tick.

As you progress through this book, you'll learn more about each case study's unique challenges and ultimately, how they achieved their goals by applying the principles in this book.

I suggest you read with a notebook at hand, so that you can complete the self-assessment, make note of key learnings, and jot ideas.

There is a seemingly unending supply of books on communication skills, so thank you again for choosing this one!

I hope you will find the information in this book as practical as I intended. It is my hope that you will find useful skills along with a few inspiring gems to help you move toward your own goals.

Enjoy!

Chapter 1: Introverts vs. Extroverts

"Extroverts organize their thoughts by talking and gain more energy by seeking outside stimuli. Introverts on the other hand, store information, reflect first, and then speak afterwards. They feel most rested and rejuvenated after they spend time alone, thinking or reading."

Marti Olsen Lany

We hear a lot about how extroverts rule the world, but is that really true?

The truth is that there are a lot of assumptions made about introverts and what makes them tick. And you may be surprised to learn who is an introvert.

Exercise: Reflect on famous people that you think may be introverts. Next, Google famous introverts to see who shows up. Were you right? Are you surprised by any names on the lists?

It is a common assumption that introverts are lacking in confidence and hate public speaking. While some may fit this profile, this is a broad generalization that is far from true. Conversely, some think that people who are confident when speaking in public must be extroverts. This is not necessarily so.

Have a look at the following summary of the characteristics of introverts and extroverts.

Characteristics of introverts:

- Restore their energy with time alone
- Prefer smaller gatherings
- Find large gatherings exhausting
- Get overwhelmed in noisy settings with multiple conversations going on
- Internal thinkers
- Need time to reflect to generate ideas and to do their best work
- Tend not to like change

Characteristics of extroverts:

- Restore their energy by being around people
- Enjoy large gatherings
- Find small gatherings boring
- Get into the spirit of meeting people, especially at a big event
- Are the only ones who will say, "The more the merrier!"
- Think out loud by talking
- Come up with ideas seemingly instantly, on the spot
- Love change

As you can see, a key difference between introverts and extroverts is how they restore their energy.

Exercise: The next time you attend any conference or other big event, observe what happens when the formal sessions are over.

Look in the bar and you will find the extroverts, restoring their energy by talking with other people. The introverts, for the most part, will be in their rooms, or out for a walk, restoring their energy by spending time alone.

Consider these common myths about introverts:

- Introverts are shy: It is an assumption that someone who is not talking is shy when, in fact, they may be deep in thought, reflecting on the subject at hand.
- Introverts don't have anything to contribute: Just because someone doesn't immediately jump into a conversation doesn't mean they have nothing to say. Perhaps they are inclined to wait until asked, or for a pause before they speak up (which may never happen) or need time to reflect.
- Introverts have social anxiety: Maybe yes or maybe no. While it is not uncommon for an introvert to experience social anxiety, not all do, and the degree certainly varies by person and situation.

You may be asking yourself, is introversion a bad thing? No, absolutely not. It is just one of the ways in which humans are different. We will look at other ways people differ in the next chapter. We are simply calling out introversion first, as this book is written to benefit introverts by offering conversation strategies specific to their unique needs.

As we wrap up this chapter, here are a few helpful caveats to keep in mind:

- While our society seemingly places a high value on extroverts, keep in mind that introverts contribute just as much to the world, if not more.
- Neither introversion nor extroversion is inherently right or wrong–these are just two different ways of being in the world.
- Learn to value what makes you tick as an introvert and carve out time to do what you need to do to take care of

yourself. If that means you need half an hour of silence to restore your energy while your extrovert co-workers are at the bar, that's fine.

- Trust your gut.
- Focus on your strengths and build on them.

What do you think? Are you an introvert?

Introversion vs. Extroversion Self-Assessment

Take a few minutes to reflect on whether you are an introvert or an extrovert.

1. What restores your energy:
a) being with people
b) time alone
2. What do you prefer:
   a) a big party
   b) a quiet dinner with a friend
3. How do you do your best thinking:
   a) out loud
   b) internally
4. How do you problem solve:
a) verbally (sharing possibilities with others)
b) internally (reflecting on possibilities as you refine them)
5. Do your best ideas:
a) come to you right away
b) come to you after you have had time to reflect
6. If you are at a gathering with multiple conversations going on at the same time, are you:
a) energized by the buzz
b) overwhelmed by the noise
7. If you are attending a conference, do you tend to:
a) mingle with and meet lots of people
b) keep to yourself
8. What best describes your ability to concentrate? Are you:
a) easily distracted

b) able to concentrate for long stretches of time
9. Do you share personal information about yourself with:
   a) just about anyone
   b) just close family and friends
10. What best describes how you feel about change. Do you:
    a) love it
    b) resist it

If you answered the first option (a) more than the second option (b), you are probably an extrovert. That's ok. While this book isn't written specifically for you, you'll probably find you still get plenty of ideas from it.

If you answered the second option (b) more than the first option (a), you are probably an introvert. Great, this book is written for you!

Case Studies

- Rebecca never really thought of herself as an introvert, but that changed after she learned that introverts need time alone to restore their energy. That'd be her!
- Larry has always thought of himself as outgoing, but supposes he is an introvert because he likes lots of time alone and is very analytic.
- Chris knows she is definitely an introvert. There's no hiding it!
- Kelly knows he is an extrovert and he is ok with that.

Chapter 2: Understanding People

"The most important thing in communication is hearing what isn't said."

-Peter F. Drucker

We've touched on introversion versus extroversion already.

Now we will explore other ways in which people differ.

When you are aware of the many ways in which people differ, you will be better equipped to understand what makes them tick, allowing you to adapt your approach in order to have better communications.

The Gender Gap - Exercise

Which gender would you associate the following with?

Men/women:

- Use communication to create connections
- Use communication to achieve tangible outcomes
- Aim to build understanding

- Want to feel needed, appreciated and admired
- Have an underlying desire to establish dominance
- See the purpose of conversation as a means to share ideas and feelings
- See conversations as an opportunity to offer advice
- Tend to be more expressive
- Value differences
- Are less likely to interrupt
- Tend to be more rational
- Are driven to avoid failure
- Seek to impress listeners
- May offer solutions simply to avoid further discussions
- In conflict situations, will seek empathy and understanding
- Deal with stress by withdrawing

Were the answers obvious to you? Or not?

Keep your thoughts on this in mind, as we will return to gender differences shortly.

Introversion vs. Extroversion

Here is a summary of the key differences between introverts and extroverts outlined in Chapter 1.

Introverts:

- Restore their energy with time alone.
- Prefer smaller gatherings over large ones.
- Are internal thinkers and need time to reflect.

Extroverts:

- Restore their energy by being around people.
- Enjoy the stimulation of large gatherings.
- Think out loud and can come up with new ideas on the spot.

An awareness of whether you are dealing with an introvert or extrovert will allow you to adapt your approach. For example, you won't be surprised if an extrovert wants to share their ideas all at once, whereas you should allow an introvert time to reflect before answering.

Gender Differences

Women and men differ in many ways, including differences in needs, goals and values.

The following are generalizations about how each gender communicates.

You may find the gender differences feel obvious to you or you may find you resist the categorization between the sexes. This is natural. Few people are entirely one way or the other. Consider the growing acceptance of variances along the gender scale.

Regardless, an awareness of tendencies that are both innate and those developed as a result of societal norms can help you in your communications with others.

Generally speaking, women:

- Aim to build understanding and avoid isolation.
- Are relationship-oriented.
- Are synergistic (having common goals).
- Prefer equality and symmetry.
- Value the cooperation, similarities, closeness and the communications process itself.
- Want to feel cherished and respected.
- Seek understanding.
- Use communication to create connections and establish relationships.
- See the purpose of conversation to build intimacy and as a means to share ideas and feelings.

- Tend to be more expressive, talkative, polite, tentative, emotional and social than men.
- Are less likely to interrupt and swear than men.
- Deal with stress by talking about the source of stress.
- In conflict situations, seek empathy and understanding.

In general, men:

- Aim to establish dominance, impress others, be seen as a leader and avoid failure.
- Are goal- and results-oriented.
- Are adversarial (having conflicting goals).
- Prefer inequality and asymmetry.
- Value independence and differences.
- Want to feel needed, appreciated and admired.
- Seek control.
- Use communication to exert dominance and achieve tangible outcomes.
- See the purpose of conversation as a means to transmit information and offer advice.
- Tend to be more rational, unemotional, assertive and power hungry than women.
- Are more likely to interrupt or swear than women.
- Are more likely to offer solutions simply to avoid further discussion than women.
- Deal with stress by withdrawing.
- In conflict situations, will offer solutions for quick resolution.

Emotional States

Our emotional state impacts how we communicate in the moment.

Think of yourself for a moment: if you are generally easy going in your communications, might you respond differently when under a lot of stress?

Here are some emotional states to be aware of:

- People think and respond differently when they are under stress. The greater the stress, the shorter the attention span. Patience and tolerance for others slip.
- Someone who is sick or is sleep-deprived will not be at their best.
- A person who is angry isn't able to think rationally. When we are angry, our fight or flight instincts are activated. In this state, blood rushes to our extremities, far away from our brains, leaving us unequipped mentally. Expecting someone to make good decisions or communicate well when angry is foolish.
- Grief can cause someone to lose their grounding, impacting their ability to think clearly, plan, work productively and communicate with others. People grieve differently over a long time, so take personal losses into consideration.
- Other emotional states to consider include sadness, trauma or even extreme joy.

All can impact one's ability to communicate and interact with others.

Cultural Differences

People from different cultural backgrounds have many differences, ranging from beliefs, upbringing, cultural norms, life experiences, and communication skills.

Chapter 6: Non-Verbal Communications will explore cultural differences that are communicated non-verbally.

Personality Types

We are not all the same. Aside from the differences already mentioned, you know this instinctively.

Two people brought up the same, in similar circumstances, may vary in how they think and act. One person is laid back, while another never sits still. One person is casual about deadlines, while another is deadline-driven. One person coasts through life, happy with their circumstances, while another pursues their goals with dedication. None are right, and none are wrong; they are just personality differences. That said, to be effective you need to adapt your approach with each type to get your message across.

Chapter 7: Adapting to Type will provide strategies for different personality types.

As we wrap up this chapter, here are a few helpful caveats to keep in mind:

- Be open to the reality that gender differences may play.
- Make allowances for the fact that we don't know what is going on with others in any given moment.
- Look for highly emotional states and steer clear or leave lots of room for misunderstandings and reworking.
- Do not try to rationalize with an angry person.
- Be aware of possible cultural differences (more on this in Chapter 6. Non-Verbal Communications).
- It is important to adapt your approach to different types of people (more on this in Chapter 7: Adapting to Type).

What do you think? Do you have a pretty good sense of how people differ? Or are those differences a mystery to you?

Case Studies

- Rebecca finds it challenging to communicate ideas on the spot with others who are concise and fast thinkers. She needs time to reflect.
- Kelly does not know how to respond to people in heightened emotional states (upset, angry) in the workplace.
- Chris is troubled by her boss who is very task-oriented. The situation had been causing Chris to become flustered.

- Kelly is curious about how gender differences impact conversations.

Chapter 3: Communication Really Does Matter

Consider this story: Peggy was at an international conference and made time to visit the newcomer's reception, as she wanted to meet a few new people. The room was pretty busy, and most people were chatting, so she busied herself getting a nibble. With a glass of wine in her right hand, she examined the table of snacks. As soon as she had a few slices of cheese wrapped in a napkin in her left hand, another participant approached the table and introduced himself, 'Oh, this cheese selection looks fantastic, mind if I join you? I'm Mo.' Not really thinking, Peggy stuck the cheese packet into her right hand, which was already balancing her glass of wine, laughed, and reached out her left hand in response. 'Sorry, wrong hand, but all the cheese got me excited too! Nice to meet you, Mo. I'm Peggy.' She was a little surprised by the look that overcame her new friend's face and wondered why he faltered before speaking again. Peggy had been unaware that in some parts of the world, the left hand was only used for bodily functions, and never for food or touching others. By presenting her left hand, she had made an offensive gesture.

Faux Pas - Exercise

Take a moment to reflect on Peggy's story.

How could Peggy have avoided this faux pas, or embarrassing social blunder?

Communication is central to our lives.

Whether verbal or non-verbal, spoken or electronic, sighted or blind, no matter how you do it, communication is at the heart of our lives and how we interact with the world.

Communication is such a broad topic that it can be hard to narrow it down to just a few points to begin an exploration, so let's pause to look at why communication matters.

Communication Matters

Communication really does matter.

Here are some of the ways communication matters in day to day life.

Communication helps you:

- Get your ideas across
- Provide and receive feedback
- Feel heard
- Connect with people
- Contribute to your community

Faux Pas - Possibilities

Let's return to Peggy's story.

If Peggy had an awareness of cultural differences in non-verbal communication, she may have been able to avoid her blunder.

Granted, you can't be expected to know every cultural difference around the world, at least in your day-to-day work, however Peggy *was* going to an international conference. Had Peggy learned about cultural differences and refreshed herself on variances in what non-verbal cues mean, she could have avoided this embarrassing moment for herself and for the person she met.

This is a great example of how improving your communication skills can benefit you.

Benefits of Improving Your Communication Skills

Just for Introverts

While everyone can benefit from improving their communication skills, there are some very specific ways that this can help you as an introvert:

- As an introvert, you are already adept at reading a room and picking up on non-verbal cues. With a little knowledge on what to look for, you can be a powerhouse.
- Similarly, introverts are naturally great listeners. When you intentionally apply yourself to learning active listening skills, you will take your natural abilities to a higher level.
- Writing is another common strength of introverts. If you add a bit of structure, by learning how to hone your writing skills, and apply them regularly, you will contribute a lot to those around you. You'll also feel more fulfilled.

For Anyone

There are many more benefits that anyone can realize by enhancing their communication skills. Here are just a few.

Improving your communication skills can help you:

- Be more confident
- Achieve better results
- Have more influence
- Understand others

- Collaborate with others
- Achieve your goals
- Feel empowered
- Avoid embarrassing moments
- Reduce anxiety
- Increase overall life satisfaction
- Deepen your connections
- Become more compassionate
- Help others
- Make a difference in your community

As we wrap up this chapter, here are a few helpful caveats to keep in mind:

- You already have numerous strengths–celebrate what you do well!
- You'll have many ideas about how you can improve your communication skills. Jot them down but pick just a few to work on first. Don't overwhelm yourself.
- Celebrate your victories, big and small!

What do you think? Do you see how your communication skills are impacting your work, relationships and your life? Can you see benefits to improving your skills?

Case Studies

- Rebecca is disappointed that she isn't able to share her ideas or doesn't feel heard when she does. As she wants to advance her career, she is looking for solutions.
- Larry knows he is on the cusp of being really great at his job but is aware that he does not always communicate effectively. His goal this year is to converse with ease in networking situations.
- Chris feels she has a lot to contribute, but her environment is not allowing her to be heard. She wants to figure out a way

to share her ideas and figures conversation skills are a good place to start.

• Kelly believes he would be more effective and a better friend if he better understand his introverted friends and colleagues.

Chapter 4: Social Anxiety

"Shy people fear negative judgment, while introverts simply prefer less stimulation; shyness is inherently painful, and introversion is not. But in a society that prizes the bold and the outspoken, both are perceived as disadvantages."

Susan Cain

The Shy Introvert

As this chapter's opening quote says so well, being shy is not the same as being an introvert.

You might be a shy introvert, but you might not be shy at all. You just may keep to yourself.

Let the label go and be yourself.

The Anxious Introvert

Introverts have social anxiety?

Maybe yes, or maybe no.

While it is not uncommon for an introvert to experience social anxiety, not all do, and the degree certainly varies by person and situation.

There is a tendency for anxiety to build up over time. An introvert experiencing social anxiety may cause others, or even themselves, to begin to think of these to be one and the same, but it does not have to be this way.

The Easiest Way for Introverts to Reduce Anxiety

This one may surprise you, but it is good news.

As an introvert, you may find that your greatest stresses are the result of trying to live your life according to what extroverts like.

Workplaces, meetings and social settings can be loud, lack privacy and leave no time to think. The things that introverts need to survive and thrive (e.g. quiet, time to reflect and time alone) are often missing from these environments.

If you create quiet, privacy and time alone each day, you may find yourself less anxious.

Yes, it can be as simple as that.

If it sounds too simple, try it.

If you need more, that's ok, but it's a foundation.

Expecting yourself, as an introvert, to not experience stress in loud places where you get no time to think, let alone to be alone, is unreasonable.

What Else You Can Do

Here are a few other things you can do that may help you reduce your anxiety:

- Get enough sleep.

- Eat well and avoid too much caffeine.
- Arrive early at events.
- Have an exit plan.
- Give yourself permission to leave.
- Take a time out.
- Remind yourself to breathe.
- Focus outward on someone else, versus inward on yourself.
- Find one person that you can talk to and ask them a great question that will keep them talking.

Butterflies - Exercise

How do you make your butterflies fly in formation?

Take a few minutes to write down the things you currently do to reduce your anxiety.

Put big ★ stars ★next to the ones that make the biggest difference.

Draw some butterflies if you wish.

Now add to your list the suggestions from this chapter that you would like to try.

Draw some caterpillars if you wish.

These are your future butterflies, and you *can* teach them to fly in formation.

As we wrap up this chapter, here are a few helpful caveats to keep in mind:

- Give yourself permission to take a break or step away from any situation that causes you to feel anxiety.
- Planning ahead by preparing yourself for events and activities can help to decrease your anxiety.
- If you continue to experience social anxiety that is not manageable, consider a support group, therapist or life coach for assistance.

• Chapter 14: Emergencies has tips on what to do if you have an emergency such as becoming overwhelmed or having a panic attack in a social setting.

• Chapter 16: Self-Care for Introverts has tips for taking care of oneself as an introvert, many of which will also be supportive if you are experiencing social anxiety.

• When you give yourself what you need as an introvert, your anxiety may naturally decrease, as you won't be pushing yourself into uncomfortable zones.

What do you think? Do you experience a high level of social anxiety? Do you experience anxiety in all situations or just a few? Is your anxiety extreme or manageable? How would relieving some of your anxiety benefit you?

Case Studies

• Rebecca's social anxiety is a major factor preventing her from contributing to discussions at work. She is determined to turn the situation around.

• Larry's social anxiety mainly comes into play in business networking situations, where he gets tongue-tied. He'd like to become more skilled so that he could reach higher sales targets.

• Chris experiences occasional bouts of extreme anxiety at work, interspersed with mild anxiety. She'd like to lower her stress level without changing jobs.

• Kelly doesn't experience anxiety, per se, but occasionally finds his confidence waning. He'd like to understand what is going on when that happens and work it out.

Chapter 5: Communication Fundamentals

"Introverts are naturally adept when it comes to actively listening. We tend to be the friend or colleague you can call on when you're upset, or you have good news to share. We're going to be able to listen and be with you in that, without turning it around and making it about us."

Beth Buelow

We all know communication is important. Why else would you have bought this book? In this chapter, we will look at communication fundamentals–the core aspects of effective communications.

Let's begin by breaking down the elements of communication.

Slicing Up the Communications Pie

Here's some food for thought to start.

Consider the following and try to fill in the percentages:

What percentage of a message is conveyed by:

- The words spoken: ___%
- Tone of voice: ___%

- Body language: ___%

Jot down your best guesses and keep them in mind as we progress. We'll reveal the answer shortly.

Let's start our discussion on the communication fundamentals by 'listening in' on a few business leaders in their day-to-day worlds, speaking to their employees.

The Leaders Share Strategy

What do you imagine about what each speaker feels about the message they are conveying?

Gerry is speaking about the new direction for the company. His voice is upbeat. His body stance is relaxed as he speaks to the audience.

Geraldine is making a presentation about the company's new business strategy. Her voice is strained. She is seated with her arms crossed as she is speaking to the audience.

Gerhard is sharing the company's new mission statement. He is speaking clearly but sternly. His back is to the audience as he is reading the slides.

Gloria is unveiling the company's new product line. She is speaking cheerfully and clearly. She stands and holds each new product up in front of her as she discusses its features.

Grace is announcing the company's new overtime policy. Her voice is even but a bit quiet. Her head is down as she is reading the details aloud.

With the small amount of information provided, what do you imagine each speaker feels about the message they are conveying? Would you feel more confident in your response if you could hear the speaker's voice? What if you were actually in the room?

10/40/50

Here is the breakdown of roughly what percentage of a message is conveyed by the words, tone of voice, and body language.

Messages are conveyed by:

- The words spoken: 10%
- Tone of voice: 40%
- Body language: 50%

More specifically:

- About 10 % of a message is conveyed by the words spoken. While spoken words are extremely important, their meaning can be distorted if the other elements communicate a contrary message.
- About 40% of a message is conveyed by tone of voice. A voice tone that is loud, quiet, stern, cheerful, low, high, fast or slow will affect what the listener hears from the speaker.
- About 50% of a message is conveyed by body language. Body language that conveys openness (uncrossed arms, eye contact, smiling) will cause a listener to take in a different message than the same words spoken with closed body language (arms crossed, no eye contact, frown).

You may have seen studies with slightly different percentages, perhaps from famous studies in the 1960s, but the principles are essentially the same: words matter, but tone of voice and body language can distort the message if they are not aligned.

Are you surprised at all by these numbers?

Think for a moment about a time when you walked into a room in which someone later communicated a negative message. Did you pick up on anything in the person's body language that told you that something was wrong?

Think about a time when your boss had to give you negative news, either you were being laid off, or there was a performance concern.

Were there cues in your boss's body language, in how he or she was standing or sitting? What about their facial expression? When they began to speak, was it clear to you that this wasn't going to be good news? What told you that, even if they were just greeting you? More than likely, their tone of voice foretold a bit of what was to come.

The words, of course, told the full story, but in these situations rarely is the fact that it's not good news a surprise by the time the speaker gets down to the message itself.

The 10/40/50 percentages carry these lessons when communicating a message to others:

> • Words are important, but they count less than you might think IF you send a different message non-verbally.
>
> • Body language is very powerful and can dominate a message.
>
> • If body language carries a message contrary to the words you use, then the intent of your message may not be believed or may not even be heard.
>
> • Tone of voice is worth paying attention to.
>
> • It is important to be congruent, as in your words, tone of voice and body language need to send the same message.

On the other hand, the 10/40/50 percentages offer clues when interpreting messages from others:

> • If you are discomforted by a message, try to notice what signals you are picking up on: the words, the tone of voice or the speaker's body language.
>
> • Be aware that the speaker may not even be aware that they are sending conflicting messages.
>
> • Remember that you may respond instinctively to voice tone and body language, and not even be aware of it.
>
> • If you notice that the message is not congruent, you have an opportunity to ask questions or otherwise determine what the real message is.

- In most cases, you do not need to act in the moment, but should reflect on what you believe the whole message to have been.

We will delve more into non-verbal communication skills in the next chapter.

In this chapter, we will focus on listening and questioning skills.

Listening Skills

The best conversationalists put as much effort into how they listen as to what they say.

The best conversationalists:

- Listen actively to the speaker.
- Make eye contact.
- Use non-verbal communication to signal understanding (nodding).
- Ask open questions.
- Respectfully allow the other person to finish.

Active Listening

As introduced earlier, as an introvert, you are naturally a good listener. When you apply yourself to learning active listening skills, you will be well positioned to take your natural abilities to a higher level.

Active listening refers to consciously paying attention to the speaker.

With active listening:

- You give the speaker your full attention.
- You concentrate on the speaker's words.
- You pay attention to non-verbal cues.
- You make a point of not allowing yourself to be distracted.
- You do NOT think about your response.
- You do NOT guess what the person means.

- You do NOT interrupt.
- You do NOT offer contrary information
- If the person says something you believe is incorrect, or you do not understand, you WAIT until they have finished speaking.

Afterward, before responding, you ensure that you understand all of what the person has said. To do this:

- You ask clarifying questions.
- You summarize to confirm understanding.

If you feel you would like to take notes, at the beginning of the conversation you can say, "I hope you don't mind if I take a few notes. I don't want to forget anything you are saying." Then just take brief notes, as needed.

The benefits of active listening are:

- There are fewer misunderstandings.
- The speaker feels heard.
- You are more likely to be listened to afterward.
- Conflict is avoided.

The opposite of Active Listening is lazy listening, in which you pay little attention to what the other person is saying, think about what you will say in response, interrupt, don't pay attention to non-verbal communication or otherwise ignore the larger context. Lazy listening is ineffective! Ask yourself: Are you a Lazy Listener?

Your Last Vacation - Exercise

Ask a person to tell you about their last vacation. Use active listening skills as they respond.

As you listen:

- Don't allow yourself to interrupt.
- Ask questions only when the other person has stopped speaking.

- STAY CURIOUS – keep asking more questions until you really have the whole story.
- Don't interrupt to share your experiences.
- Keep going until you have learned 5 things about the person and/or their vacation.

How did you do? Did you find yourself thinking ahead or wanting to interrupt?

Questioning

Have a look at these questions. What do you notice?

"Is this your first time here?"

"Do you like raisins?"

"Have you eaten rice cakes before?"

"What is that outside the window?"

"What type of cake do you prefer?"

"What's your favorite type of pasta?"

Need a hint?

What do you notice about the first three questions as opposed to the last three questions?

The first three questions are what are referred to as "closed questions".

The last three questions are what are referred to as "open questions".

What differentiates them is the type of answer they will solicit.

The Difference Between Open and Closed Questions

Closed questions invite one-word responses, which tends to 'close' down discussion.

Open questions, on the other hand, invite the listener to respond freely, which will naturally 'open' up discussion. Open questions open the door to dialog.

To enhance your conversation skills, you need to ask more open questions than closed questions.

EXERCISE:

Identify which of the following questions are closed vs. open questions:

"Do you like Italian food?"

"What are your boys doing for the summer?"

"Are your children boys or girls, or some of each?"

"Have you been to one of these networking events before?"

"What do you like best about this type of networking event?"

"Do you have anything to add to the discussion?"

"What do you have to add to the discussion?"

"Did you like this morning's speaker?"

"What did you think of this morning's speaker?"

Are Closed Questions Bad?

Closed questions are those that can be answered with "Yes", "No" or a single word answer, such as "Boys", "Three", "Tomorrow".

Are closed questions bad?

No, not necessarily, but they have their place.

Closed questions can be handy for getting quick answers to simple questions or for collecting information quickly. For example:

"Can you hear me at the back?"

"Can you see over me?"

"Do you want coffee or tea?"

"What day is your dental appointment?"

"Will you be in tomorrow?"

What other situations can you think of where closed questions might be most appropriate?

Create your own list but remember, to become an effective conversationalist, you need to master open questions.

Open Questions

An open question is any question that elicits an answer of longer than a single word.

The reason that open questions are preferred over closed questions is that open questions engage the other person and begin a dialogue.

EXERCISE:

You are at a conference and are waiting in line to get a coffee after a morning of speakers. What are three open questions you could ask your fellow delegates?

1.

2.

3.

Tip: *You will probably quickly see how easy it is to fall into the trap of asking a closed question rather than an open one.*

As open questions really can be your SECRET WEAPON though, it's worth spending time mastering this skill.

Open questions are a BIG ADVANTAGE that introverts can have over extroverts when meeting people.

Why?

Most introverts:

- Prefer one-on-one conversations over speaking with groups.

- Would rather have a nice long chat with one person than make a lot of small talk with many people.
- Like interesting people.

As a result, mastering open questions can truly be the key to lowering your anxiety and having engaging discussions with the people you meet.

Yes, extroverts can ask open questions too, but they may very well have already flitted onto the next person, not concerned about how deeply they have connected with the person they just met. While they are off looking for the party, you can be having meaningful conversations.

And people WILL want to talk to you.

When you ask questions that engage others, they will want to share with you.

People love to talk about themselves, so if you present yourself with confidence, have a great greeting and ask open questions of the people you meet, you will find yourself engaged in conversation.

For this reason, mastering open questions can be your SECRET KEY to getting people to talk.

From Closed to Open - Exercise

Rewrite these closed questions as open questions.

For example:

"Do you want to go for lunch today?" – closed question

"Where do you want to go for lunch today?" – open question

"Did you like this morning's speaker?"

"Are you going away for Christmas?"

"Do you play a musical instrument?"

"Are you just visiting?"

"Do you have any ideas to add?"

"Are there any questions?"

"Do you like kayaking?"

"Did you have a good vacation?"

"Do you like to travel?"

"Did you enjoy college?"

"Do you want me to phone you?"

"Do you like sunny days?"

"Do you like to go for long drives?"

"Do you like juice?"

"You've met Sally before, right?"

Possible Responses

How did you make out?

Here are some examples of how these closed questions can be transformed into open questions:

"Did you like this morning's speaker?"

"What did you think of this morning's speaker?"

"How did you like this morning's speaker?"

"What did you like best about this morning's speaker?"

"Are you going away for Christmas?"

"Where are you going for Christmas?"

"What are you doing for Christmas?"

"Do you play a musical instrument?"

"What musical instruments do you play?"

"Are you just visiting?"

"Where are you visiting from?"

"Do you have any ideas to add?"

"What ideas do you have to add?"

"Are there any questions?"

"What questions do you have?"

"What questions are there?"

"Do you like kayaking?"

"What do you like about kayaking?"

"What water sports do you like?"

"Did you have a good vacation?"

"What was the best part about your vacation?"

"Tell me about your vacation."

"Do you like to travel?"

"What types of travel do you like to do?"

"Tell me about your travel experiences."

"Did you enjoy college?"

"What did you enjoy about college?"

"What was college like for you?"

"Do you want me to phone you?"

"How do you want me to follow up with you?"

"Do you like sunny days?"

"What do you like to do on sunny days?"

"Do you like to go for long drives?"

"If you had time today for a long drive, where would you go?"

"Do you like juice?"

"What is your favorite type of juice?"

"You've met Sally before, right?"

"When and how did you meet Sally?"

Leading Questions

Have a look at this next set of questions and see what you notice?

"Do you want to go for lunch today?"

"Do you want to go to Ben's Burger's for lunch?"

"Where do you want to go for lunch today?"

You will probably have recognized the first and second questions as being closed questions, and the last question as being an open question. But what is different about the second question?

Clue: What do you think the questioner wants to hear in response?

The second question is what is referred to as a 'leading' question

"Do you want to go for lunch today?" – closed question

"Do you want to go to Ben's Burger's for lunch?" – leading question

"Where do you want to go for lunch today?" – open question

A leading question is any question in which you 'telegraph' your desired response.

For example:

"You like working at this office, right?"

"We had a great time at the party, didn't we?"

"What are the worst parts of working Saturdays?"

The reason that leading questions are not desirable is that they are not getting at what the other person thinks. They are actually manipulative, though generally without malicious intent. And they aren't going to help you become an accomplished conversationalist.

From Leading to Open - Exercise

Rewrite these leading questions into non-leading open questions.

"Do you have conflicts with your supervisor?"

"How fast was the Mercedes going before it hit the BMW?"

"Don't you hate flying?"

"Well, that was a great seminar, wasn't it?"

"How much time will the new process save you?"

"Did you have a good day at school?"

"How was your awesome vacation?"

"Did you like our new styles?"

"Did you enjoy the team-building activity?"

"You have a great boss, don't you?"

"Wasn't that movie exciting?"

"What parts of the new software are the hardest to adapt to?"

Possible Responses

How did you make out with these questions?

Here are some possibilities of how these leading questions can be transformed into open questions:

"Do you have conflict with your supervisor?"

"What is your relationship like with your supervisor?"

"How fast was the Mercedes going before it hit the BMW?"

"How fast was each car going before they collided?"

"Don't you hate flying?"

"How you do you find flying?"

"Well, that was a great seminar, wasn't it?"

"What did you think of the seminar?"

"How much time will the new process save you?"

"How will the new processes affect your productivity?"

"Did you have a good day at school?"

"What was your day at school like today?"

"How was your awesome vacation?"

"How was your vacation?"

"What was the highlight of your vacation?"

"Did you like our new styles?"

"What was your reaction to our new styles?"

"Did you enjoy the team-building activity?"

"What did you think of the team-building activity?"

"You have a great boss, don't you?"

"What's your boss like?"

"Wasn't that movie exciting?"

"What did you think of that movie?"

"What parts of the new software are the hardest to adapt to?"

"What has your experience been adapting to the new software?"

As we wrap up this chapter, here are a few helpful caveats to keep in mind:

- As an introvert, you are naturally a good listener. As you apply yourself to learning active listening skills, you will be beginning to take your natural abilities to a higher level.
- Messages are conveyed by the words spoken (10%), tone of voice (40%) and body language (50%).
- Use active listening by giving the speaker your full attention.

- Ask more open questions than closed questions.
- Avoid leading questions that 'telegraph' the desired answer.
- Non-verbal communication carries a powerful message (more on this next in Chapter 6).
- Voice tone also matters (more on this in Chapter 11).

What do you think? After learning about the fundamentals, what do you think your strengths are? Where are your biggest opportunities for improvement?

Case Studies

- Rebecca found the techniques of clarifying and summarizing to be most helpful. Not only did she find she understood more when she took time to clarify, but summarizing conversations led to her being asked to summarize meetings, which allowed her to structure opportunities for her own input to be heard.
- Larry found the active listening to be a particularly helpful skill, not only at work but at home as well. Forcing himself to put down his phone, and stop thinking ahead immediately resulted in more revealing conversations and deeper connections with loved ones.
- Chris was delighted to learn that she could substitute open questions for closed questions and keep the other person talking longer!
- Kelly was astounded at how many leading questions he used to ask. When he stopped using them, he noticed people shared a lot more with him.

The Introvert's Survival Guide to Active Listening

Active listening is the key to people feeling heard and to you getting the full story from a person.

Here are a few do's and don'ts to keep in mind:

Do's

DO listen to what the other person is saying.

DO pay attention to their words, their tone of voice and their body language.

DO give cues that you are listening (eye contact, nodding).

DO ask clarifying questions.

DO summarize to check understanding.

Don'ts

DON'T think about your response while the other person is speaking.

DON'T interrupt the person you are listening to.

DON'T have an agenda.

3 Keys to Remember

KEY 1: Use active listening.

KEY 2: Don't think about your response.

KEY 3: Pay attention to the whole message.

The Introvert's Survival Guide to Asking Questions

Your ability to ask thoughtful open questions is your best tool for getting people to open up to you.

Here are a few do's and don'ts to keep in mind:

Do's

DO ask open questions.

DO think ahead about the questions you will ask.

DO ask follow-up questions.

DO use active listening.

DO take a few notes, if needed.

Don'ts

DON'T ask closed questions.

DON'T 'telegraph' the answer you are seeking by asking leading questions.

3 Keys to Remember

KEY 1: Use open questions and avoid closed or leading questions.

KEY 2: Listen actively to the answers.

KEY 3: If in doubt, ask another question.

Chapter 6: Non-Verbal Communication

"The typical introvert uses his or her observant nature to read the room. They're more likely to notice people's body language and facial expressions, which makes them better at interpersonal communication."

Dr. Jennifer Kahnweiler

In the last chapter, we learned that messages are conveyed by the words spoken (10%), the tone of voice (40%) and body language (50%).

In this chapter, we will look at the body language aspect of this equation, also referred to as non-verbal communication skills.

As mentioned earlier, as an introvert, you are already adept at reading a room and picking up on non-verbal cues. With just a little more knowledge on what to look for, you truly can be a powerhouse.

Non-Verbal Communication Cues

What do you think the following might mean? If you can think of more than one possibility, write them all down.

Arms crossed

Legs crossed

Knee bouncing

Body turned away

Making eye contact

Not making eye contact

Rolling eyes

Eyes wandering

Eyes closed

Looking toward the door

Looking at the floor

Looking at a watch

Chewing on a pen

Fingers tapping rhythmically

Tapping a single finger

Pointing a finger

Clenched fists

Standing up

Pacing

Slumping in a chair

Leaning back in a chair

Pounding the table

Standing at a distance

Standing very close

Pushing

We will return to the list later, but in the meantime, keep these in mind as you read this chapter.

Gestures

What do you the following gestures mean to you? Are you aware of alternate meanings in other cultures? Are there any you would avoid?

Thumbs up

Palm up and forward

Hand up with fingers spread

Finger and thumb together, forming a circle

Single finger curled towards you, beckoning

Index and baby finger up, middle fingers down

Fist with thumb poking out between the index and second finger

Snapping fingers

We will return to cultural differences later, and these gestures in particular. In the meantime, if more possible meanings come to you, jot them down.

Why Body Language Matters

About 50% of the message one hears is the from the speaker's non-verbal messages. These include eye contact (or lack thereof), arms crossed, chair pushed back, head down, looking away, rolling eyes, rigid back, laid back in the chair, legs crossed (or uncrossed), standing, or sitting.

Some are considered universal (e.g. arms crossed, lack of eye contact), whereas others are particular to the individual (e.g. a person who usually sits stands, or sitting upright when usually laid back).

You have to consider the situation (could the person with their arms crossed simply be cold?) and how well you know the person.

As a general rule, however, these non-verbal cues may not come to you consciously, at least not at first. Your body may react to non-verbal signals before you've even had a chance to think about them.

The same applies to the speaker's tone of voice, which accounts for 40% of the message conveyed. More often than not, your psyche will respond to any tension in the speaker's tone of voice before you have even had a chance to think about it. You may find yourself feeling guarded before you've even heard the essence of the spoken message.

Of course, words are important, but at 10%, you don't want to ignore the power of what you communicate non-verbally at 50%, and the message sent by the tone of your voice, at 40%, as factors in how your entire message comes across.

Body Language for Introverts

Beyond reading the body language of others, there are numerous benefits to monitoring to your own body language.

Paying attention to your body language will help you:

- Appear more confident
- Feel more confident
- Reduce your anxiety
- Boost your testosterone

This is especially good news for introverts.

When your anxiety is reduced, your focus will turn outward. And when your attention is directed outside of yourself, you will break the anxiety spiral.

Take a breath and enjoy the experience, as in this improved state you will find yourself having more enriching conversations with others.

Open Body Stance

The key is to adopt an open body stance with an erect posture, standing tall, with your head up, shoulders back and elbows out.

This posture is referred to as 'open' as, in a primitive context, your body is more exposed. In a battle, you would be more vulnerable.

A few hints:

- Keep your arms uncrossed. If your arms are crossed, you will begin to feel more anxious. Uncrossing your arms will actually reduce your anxiety.
- Plant your feet firmly on the ground, far enough apart to secure your balance. Resist the temptation to balance on one foot or lean against something.
- Hold your elbows out from your body. Take up as much room as possible. If you are holding a wine glass, practice holding it away from your body.
- Use hand gestures while you are speaking.
- When you are talking with someone, nod your head to indicate interest. A 'triple nod' when someone stops speaking will be a signal that you'd like them to continue (try it, it works).
- Resist the temptation to check your phone, as you will immediately take on a closed stance, and repel people from you (more on this later in the chapter).

The result of standing with your elbows out and using hand gestures is that your body will physically take up more space. The more space your body takes up, the more confidence you will exude.

You may recognize this posture in speakers and other people with significant personal power. This is what is referred to as a power position, but it doesn't necessarily mean you are seeking power. Rather, you appear confident.

Now let's return to what messages our body language sends to others.

Non-Verbal Communication Cues – A Few Possibilities

Earlier in the chapter, you guessed what a number of non-verbal communication cues might mean. Get out your notes and compare your ideas with the possibilities below.

Arms crossed – might mean:

- Defensive
- Closed to listening
- Cold and trying to warm oneself

Legs crossed – might mean:

- Relaxed
- Defensive
- Physical discomfort

Knee bouncing – might mean:

- Impatience
- Nervous energy
- Excitement

Body turned away crossed – might mean:

- Disinterested
- Closed to ideas
- Desire to flee

Making eye contact – might mean:

- Open
- Challenging (staring)
- Listening

Not making eye contact – might mean:

- Closed
- Avoiding

- Distracted
- Shame

Rolling eyes – might mean:

- Fed up
- Disagreeable

Eyes wandering – might mean:

- Distracted
- Disinterested
- Listening

Eyes closed – might mean:

- Listening
- Thinking
- Concentrating
- Avoidance
- Sleeping

Looking towards the door – might mean:

- Desire to flee
- Distracted

Looking at the floor – might mean:

- Thoughtful
- Distracted
- Shame

Looking at watch – might mean:

- Tight for time
- Distracted
- Desire to leave

Chewing on a pen – might mean:

- Listening
- Thoughtful

Fingers tapping rhythmically – might mean:

- Impatient
- Nervous habit
- Excited

Tapping a single finger – might mean:

- Trying to make a point
- Dominating
- Aggression

Pointing a finger – might mean:

- Accusing
- Authoritarian gesture
- Look there (if pointed away)

Clenched fists – might mean:

- Frustration
- Anger
- Impatience

Standing up – might mean:

- Ready to leave
- Deep in thought
- Physical discomfort

Pacing – might mean:

- Deep in thought
- Worried
- Impatience

Slumping in a chair – might mean:

- Relaxed
- Defeated
- Tired

Leaning back in a chair – might mean:

- Relaxed
- Listening

- Disinterested

Pounding the table – might mean:

- Feeling unheard
- Emphasis
- Anger

Standing at a distance – might mean:

- Disengaged
- Respectful
- Aloof

Standing very close – might mean:

- Intimidating
- Disrespectful
- Assertive

Pushing – might mean:

- Assertive
- Disrespectful
- Crowd behavior

Cultural Differences

As we have discussed, people from different cultural backgrounds can vary greatly in terms of beliefs, cultural norms and communication styles.

This is perhaps most evident in non-verbal communications.

Eye Contact

In the west, eye contact is not only common; it is expected. If someone does not make eye contact, we think they are hiding something. In other cultures, direct eye contact is seen as rude and confrontational, and avoiding eye contact is a sign of respect.

Personal Space

In the west, we expect a fair amount of personal space around us physically. If someone gets too close, we feel our personal space has been invaded, and we become uncomfortable. If there is incidental touch, we consider the offender to be rude and inconsiderate. Yet, in other cultures, such as highly populated countries, holding back and not asserting yourself physically can be considered a weakness.

Gestures

Gestures have completely different meanings depending upon the part of the world you come from.

If you were traveling, you would probably study the countries and the region you were traveling to in order to learn what gestures are and are not acceptable.

Living in a multicultural society, however, you could unintentionally insult someone you are speaking with by using a gesture that has a completely different meaning in their homeland.

Here are a few examples:

- Standing with your hands on your hips conveys confidence and pride and is considered to be a power position in the west, however this stance can be interpreted as challenging or anger.
- While winking might mean 'We share a secret,' or a romantic interest in the west, it is considered rude in some cultures. It can also be a signal for children to leave the room.
- Slouching may just be seen as lazy or relaxed in the west, but in some cultures, it is a sign of disrespect.
- Crossing one's legs, with the bottom of one foot exposed, may be meaningless in the west, but it is considered dirty and rude elsewhere in the world.
- Even nodding has different meanings. In the west, nodding your head up and down means yes, and shaking your side-to-

side means no, but there are cultures where these meanings are reversed.

Let's return to the list of gestures from earlier in this chapter.

Gestures – Different Cultural Meanings

How many of these were familiar to you? Did you know that any could be considered to be rude or insulting?

Thumbs up – in various cultures, this gesture can mean:

- That's ok
- Up yours

Palm up and forward – in various cultures, this gesture can mean:

- Stop
- Settle down
- Call a waiter

Hand up with fingers spread – in various cultures, this gesture can mean:

- Greeting
- Eat shit

Finger and thumb together, forming a circle – in various cultures, this gesture can mean:

- OK sign
- Your anus
- Zero

Single finger curled towards you, beckoning – in various cultures, this gesture can mean:

- Come here
- Rude, only used for dogs
- Death

Index and baby finger up, middle fingers down – in various cultures, this gesture can mean:

- Positive

- Sign of the devil

Fist with thumb poking out between the index and second finger – in various cultures, this gesture can mean:

- Good luck
- Fertility
- Female genitalia
- Screw you

Snapping fingers – in various cultures, this gesture can mean:

- I have an idea
- Hurry up
- Offensive

While you no one can be expected to know what every gesture might mean worldwide, it can only help your interpersonal interactions if you can avoid some common pitfalls.

Context is Everything

Of course, you can't know for sure what is going on with someone without asking them, and that is not always appropriate. So consider the signals you pick up on to be clues, not definitive answers.

On the other hand, if you know the person, you have the extra advantage of knowing what is unusual for them. In a word, you have context. Often it is your knowledge of the person that allows you to become aware of changes in body language that others would miss.

Here are a few scenarios that illustrate this point.

In each situation, what do you think might be going on? Are there any non-verbal cues that a bystander would realize are significant?

A Meeting with Marty

Angelina walked into her boss, Marty's, office. He had a big grin on his face. He was on the phone, so signaled for her to sit, covering the mouthpiece to whisper that he would only be a minute.

Fred's Meeting with Norman

Fred checked his watch and slipped into his boss, Norman's, office. Norman was on the phone, but he signaled for him to sit down. Aside from this, he did not make eye contact.

The Monday Meeting

Melinda worked remotely but called in weekly to a team meeting with her department at home office. Her colleague, Martin, answered, said they were waiting for Maria, and put Melinda on speakerphone. When she heard the project manager, Maria's, voice, apologizing for being late, Melinda put down her pen to listen. Maria cleared her throat and began the meeting. Keith reported on last week's numbers, but then before anyone else could speak Maria said, "Before we get into today's agenda…"

The RRR Rodeo Team Meeting

Ruth, Ralph, Reggie and the rest of the RRR Rodeo team gathered in the Roundup Meeting Room. When their boss, Rudy, arrived a few minutes late, he didn't say much and shuffled his papers. There were traces of a grin on Rudy's face.

The President Speaks

Nancy slipped into the meeting room late and the President was already speaking. Everyone else was quiet. There were arms crossed and pushed-back chairs.

The Family Business

Jack was part of a business founded by his father, Leo, who now left day-to-day operations to Jack, his brother, Mack, and their sister, Missy. When he got a text to return to the office for a meeting, he didn't think much about it. When he opened the conference room door, Missy, Mack and Mr. Clifton, the family's lawyer, were already seated.

Any guesses? There isn't much to go on, is there? What additional cues might someone familiar with the individuals notice?

In situations where you already know the person (versus meeting a stranger), you have the added advantage of noticing changes in behavior. For example, a co-worker whose expressive eyes you enjoy when they speak is avoiding eye contact. Or a manager who is usually very chatty in welcoming people to meetings today has his head buried in papers as everyone arrives.

Let's return to our scenarios, this time from the perspective of the participants.

In each of these scenarios, there are signals telling the listener something about what was to come. Before a word was spoken, they had a sense of what was going to happen. This time, you have the advantage of this context.

A Meeting with Marty – Angelina's perspective

Angelina walked into her boss, Marty's, office and laughed when she saw the great big grin on his face. He was like a little kid sometimes, she thought. He was on the phone, so signaled for her to sit, covering the mouthpiece to whisper that he would only be a minute. Angelina waited with anticipation, wondering what was up.

- Interpretation: Angelina figured good news was coming.
- Non-Verbal Cues: the grin on Marty's face, his body language as he signaled for Angelina to sit down.

Fred's Meeting with Norman – Fred's perspective

Fred checked his watch, slipped into his boss, Norman's, office, and took a seat. As usual, Norman was on the phone, but he signaled for him to sit down. Fred immediately felt tense, as he noticed that Norman wasn't making eye contact with him. The two had worked together for years, and Fred instinctively picked up on a change in pattern.

- Interpretation: Norman was going to tell Fred something he wasn't going to like.
- Non-Verbal Cues: Lack of usual eye contact.

The Monday Meeting – Melinda's perspective

Melinda worked remotely but called in weekly to a team meeting with her department at home office. Her colleague, Martin, picked up the phone when it rang, said "Maria's late, we're just waiting," and put Melinda on speakerphone. It was the usual Monday morning banter, which Melinda half listened to as she made her notes for the meeting. It wasn't quite the same as being there in person, but that was ok; she was used to it. When she heard the project manager, Maria's voice, apologizing for being late, Melina put down her pen to listen. The room was largely quiet as they waited for Maria to start, which she eventually did, by clearing her throat. With a more serious tone than usual, Maria began the meeting. As usual, she had Keith report on last week's numbers, then Maria jumped in before anyone could comment, and said, "Before we get into today's agenda…" Melinda was immediately alert to the seriousness in Maria's voice and held her breath.

- Interpretation: Something's up and it's not good news.
- Non-Verbal Cues: Maria clearing her throat, the way Maria jumped in before anyone could say anything, Maria's tone of voice.

The RRR Rodeo Team Meeting – Ruth's perspective

Ruth, Ralph, Reggie and the rest of RRR Rodeo team gathered in the Roundup Meeting Room, where they had been beckoned by their boss, Rudy. When Rudy arrived, a few minutes late, he didn't say much (unusual for him) and shuffled his papers, but Ruth could see the traces of a grin playing at the side of his mouth. She wondered what was up.

- Interpretation: Ruth suspected good news or some sort of surprise.
- Non-Verbal Cues: A change in behavior, and traces of a grin.

The President Speaks – Nancy's perspective

When Nancy slipped into the meeting room late, she couldn't catch the thread of the conversation, but she noticed that the President's tone of voice – usually cheery – was restrained. As she found a seat, she looked around at her colleagues and noticed a lot of crossed arms and pushed-back chairs. Uh oh, she thought, I wonder what's up.

- Interpretation: There is bad news afoot, and the others already know it.
- Non-Verbal Cues: President's tone of voice, and the body language of her colleagues.

The Family Business – Jack's perspective

Jack was part of a family-run business, founded by his father, Leo. For the most part today, Leo played a behind the scenes role and left day-to-day operations to Jack, his brother, Mack, and their sister, Missy. When he got the text to return to the office for an important meeting, he didn't think much about it. When he opened the conference room door, however, and saw Missy and Mack sitting, with stunned expressions, across from Mr. Clifton, the family's lawyer, he knew it wasn't good news.

- Interpretation: Something has happened to dad.
- Non-Verbal Cues: The stunned expressions on Missy and Mack's faces, and the presence of Mr. Clifton.

Can you now see the signals that the participants, who were familiar with the players involved, were able to notice?

This doesn't mean that you won't notice non-verbal signals from strangers. You can, but you might not always know for sure what is going on.

It's always wise to withhold judgment, but spend some time observing body language in the meetings you attend and see what you can pick up on.

Message Mismatch

What do you do if you are faced with a disconnect between what someone says and what their body language and/or tone of voice is conveying?

Take a minute to reflect.

If you notice a mismatch between what a person is saying and the other signals you are receiving, your options are either to:

- Do nothing at the moment.
- Ask a question.
- Reflect on the interaction afterward.
- Have a follow-up discussion.
- Still do nothing.

In terms of asking a question, you could ask a specific question about the mismatch or simply mirror back what you observed. Here is some wording that might work:

- "I notice you looking at your watch. Do you have another meeting? Would you like to reschedule for when you have more time?"
- "I'm interested in your feedback on what I have said so far."
- "That's what happened, from my perspective. I'd like to hear what happened from your perspective."
- "I'm picking up that you may be uncomfortable with what I am saying. Would you like to share what's on your mind?"
- "I know you are saying that you are happy with my work on the project, but you are not smiling. Is there something that is concerning you?"

A disconnect between words and non-verbal cues could be a signal that your approach is off, so reflect on the conversation afterward.

For example: If your "Here's how I saw it unfold," brought downcast eyes or crossed arms, perhaps try a different approach next time. For example, "I'd like to share what I observed first, then I'd like to hear what happened from your perspective," may bring a different reaction.

Personal Safety and De-escalating Situations

Sometimes non-verbal cues can tell you that something is seriously off. If someone is acting aggressively–such as yelling, pointing a finger at you–you may need to extricate yourself from the situation for your own safety.

It's also good to know some tricks for de-escalating a situation.

Listening is the most important thing you can do. Ask the other person for their perspective and use your active listening skills until you fully understand things from their angle. Don't disagree or try to solve the problem at this time. Just keep probing until they feel heard. When people feel heard, they are less likely to act with hostility or shut down or refuse to listen.

You might feel like you are the only one steering the boat, but that's ok.

Those Darn Smartphones

Our discussion on non-verbal communication would not be complete without a discussion on the ubiquitous cell phone.

Scrolling or typing on a Smartphone may seem rude to you, but it actually might not be.

In today's culture, many people are so attached to their devices that they can't imagine putting them down. They may believe that they can listen just as well if they are busy on their phone versus not, but not quite. But don't take this alone to be a sign of rudeness.

That said, having your nose stuck in your Smartphone is not going to help your conversation skills. The very act will shut down any possibility of meeting new people, let alone starting new conversations.

Think about what happens when we are engaged with these devices:

- What non-verbal signals do you send when you are using your device?
- What non-verbal messages have you picked up from others?
- If you are somewhere now where people are using their devices, have a look around. What do you notice about their body language?
- If you are alone right now, try this exercise when you are next out and about in the world. Look around you and observe the non-verbal messages being sent by those who are busy on their devices.
- Next time you go to a meeting or a gathering, observe the other people as they arrive. Who ends up in a conversation first--someone with their head stuck in their phone or the rare person who is waiting patiently for the meeting to begin?

Yes, if you'd rather be left alone, then you could consider your phone to be your best friend, but as you have purchased this book on conversation skills, this is probably not your goal. It may be your instinct, but it will not help you interact.

Here's what happens when you are looking at the screen on your Smartphone:

- Your head is tilted down.
- Your shoulders are naturally pulled in.
- Your attention is diverted.
- Your body language is closed.
- The signal you are sending is 'Stay away'.
- It is not possible for someone to even catch your eye.

- In a word, you are unapproachable.

By the way, any hope you might have that occupying yourself with your phone might suggest that you are very busy, have urgent messages or are otherwise more important than anyone else, is dead. Everyone knows what you are doing because they have done it themselves.

A few final tips about Smartphones:

- If you want to meet people, put your phone down. Put it away. Turn it off or put it in silent mode.
- When you find yourself alone at an event with no one to talk to, resist the temptation to look at your phone.
- If you need to check your phone, step aside and do it, then put it away.

Finally, don't let your phone become a crutch. It's far too easy to cover awkward silences by retreating into your device but resist the temptation. You just might find someone interesting to talk to!

As we wrap up this chapter, here are a few helpful caveats to keep in mind:

- As an introvert, you are already adept at picking up on non-verbal cues; keep on learning–you are on your way to becoming a powerhouse.
- Keep in mind that a person could have their arms crossed because they are cold, but it could mean something else too.
- Reading body language is looking for clues but is not definitive.
- Trust your gut. If you get a strong feeling something is amiss, it probably is.
- Context is everything. If you know the person and/or the surrounding circumstances, take this into account when interpreting body language.
- Consider your own body language.

- Body language can mean different things in different cultures.
- Voice tone also matters (more on this in Chapter 11).

What do you think? Do you notice other people's non-verbal communications? Since reading this chapter, have you started noticing your own reactions to the non-verbal signals others send out? Do you notice anything you do that sends an unintended message contrary to what you intend?

Case Studies

- Rebecca knew she wore her feelings on her sleeve; there was no hiding how she felt! With a greater understanding of non-verbal communication, she was able to be intentional with her body language, so as to not be so overtly emotional in non-critical situations.
- Larry was sometimes accused of being defensive, when he didn't think he was. After learning about non-verbal communication, he was able to consciously uncross his arms and make better eye contact. Coupled with his new active listening skills, he stopped hearing this feedback.
- Chris didn't understand why everyone thought she was intimidated by others. As she gained an understanding of her body language and the signals she sent out, she was able to make some minor adjustments to appear more confident: not bowing her head, making more eye contact and nodding while listening.
- Non-verbal communication was not something Kelly had paid much attention to in the past. Initially, he became fascinated by the non-verbal messages others sent, analyzing people in all sorts of situations. Ultimately, he was able to identify that his habit of throwing down his pen when he was fed up was putting people off. Now he laid his pen down gently.

The Introvert's Survival Guide to Non-Verbal Communication

Your ability to convey open body language and read the non-verbal cues of others can go a long way to improving the effectiveness of your communications.

Here are a few do's and don'ts to keep in mind:

Do's

DO observe the body language of others.

DO be aware of your own body language.

DO use an open body stance (stand tall, shoulders apart).

DO plant your feet firmly on the ground.

DO smile.

DO make eye contact.

DO ask a question.

Don'ts

DON'T cross your arms.

DON'T beat yourself up if you fumble.

DON'T problem-solve if you are angry.

DON'T expect everyone to respond the same.

3 Keys to Remember

KEY 1: Adopt an open body stance.

KEY 2: Stay off your phone.

KEY 3: Communicate that you are approachable.

The Introvert's Survival Guide to Smartphones

Put it away. Just put it away. You don't need your Smartphone to interact with people in person.

Here are a few do's and don'ts to keep in mind:

Do's

DO put your phone away.

DO be the one person in the room who is not on a device.

Don'ts

DON'T hide behind your phone.

DON'T cover awkward pauses by pulling out your phone.

DON'T assume others on their phones are being rude.

3 Keys to Remember

KEY 1: To meet people, put your phone away.

KEY 2: Deal with any urgent matter, then put your device away.

KEY 3: Don't use your phone as a crutch.

Chapter 7: Adapting to Type

As introduced in Chapter 2: Understanding People, there are many ways in which people differ including:

- Introversion vs. extroversion
- Gender
- Emotions
- Culture
- Personality

Next, we will explore how you can adapt your approach to different types of people.

To begin, pause to think for a moment about your friends.

My Friends – Exercise

Which of your friends, family members and co-workers you would describe as being primarily results-oriented and which you would describe as laid back?

Results-oriented friends (lots of goals, achievement-focused, driven):

1.

2.

3.

4.

5.

Laid-back friends (easy going, live in the moment, tend to go with the flow)

1.

2.

3.

4.

5.

The Proposal – Exercise

You need to get four different people in your company to review and approve a proposal you are making to fund a new training program. All four senior managers are quite different from one another.

Your proposal is 16 pages long, including a 1-page executive summary, a 10-page synopsis, 1 page of measurements and 3 pages of charts showing how the new training process fit in with other aspects of the business. There is also a financial summary at the end.

In general terms, you plan to email your proposal to each of the managers then make appointments to meet with each to answer questions and get their sign-off.

Before doing so, you spend some time thinking about the four managers and how you might adapt your approach to each.

Irene is a senior manager in the purchasing department. Extremely busy and extremely bright, there are many demands on her time. Once you had her attention though, Irene would always hear you out, listening to your ideas, and giving them careful consideration. Irene has a high need for measurements and financial details and will want time to analyze the details before committing. Sitting in her office, piled high with files, you never felt rushed; the big challenge was getting enough time in her schedule to get her input.

Randy is a senior manager in the sales department. On the rare occasions when he is not away working with sales reps in the field, client meetings, and sales conferences, Randy has office days. If you wanted to see Randy, you needed to book an appointment. If you were lucky, he would be free when you got there. He'd always see you next if you'd booked an appointment, but at times there would quite literally be a lineup outside. You always felt like you were jumping the queue if he ushered you past others waiting. And there was always the possibility of an interruption, or a meeting cut short due to a client crisis of one sort or another. As a result, you always felt a bit jittery when you had a meeting with Randy.

James was a senior manager in human resources. While not quite as busy as the other managers, meeting with James was no piece of cake. He'd generously give you more time than you asked for and would be genuinely interested in your ideas, but you'd better know your stuff. James would have read every word in your proposal and would have prepared a list of questions. If your proposal was solid, you'd walk away feeling great, though the price to pay was a 10-minute chat about your career and professional goals. Those weren't hard discussions, but if you hadn't done anything towards those goals since your last little chat, you'd feel like a dolt, hence causing you to think you should research night-school classes first.

Marjorie was a senior manager in quality control. She was a key player in the company, serving on more project teams than anyone else. Plus, she had the President's ear. Other managers would frequently ask, "Has Marjorie seen this yet?", so she was well respected. You could always book time with Marjorie, and she was open to multiple meetings if you needed her input. Marjorie's office walls were covered with charts, including the systems your proposal will need to fit in with. She wasn't going to approve anything that didn't align with the quality management system and the organization's business strategy though, so you needed to be on your game.

How would you adapt your approach to each? What does each need, and how will you provide it?

Irene in Purchasing

- Needs:
- Has little time for:
- Key to getting her approval:

Randy in Sales

- Needs:
- Has little time for:
- Key to getting his approval:

James in Human Resources

- Needs:
- Has little time for:
- Key to getting his approval:

Marjorie in Quality Control

- Needs:
- Has little time for:
- Key to getting her approval:

Give some thought to these and jot some notes in your notebook. Keep Irene, Randy, James, and Marjorie in mind as we go through this chapter.

Personality Type Models

In terms of personality type, there are many models that seek to explain how we differ.

These models:

- Strive to break down the range of types, so that we can understand what makes others tick.

- Help individuals understand themselves better so they can get their needs met in a range of situations.
- Provide insight as to why someone may behave in a certain way, so that you can adapt your communication in such a way that the person is most likely to hear you and engage with you.
- Are particularly valuable to teams, as when a model is embraced, team members are better able to understand each other, allowing them to get the most out of their interactions and effectively work together to maximize results.

Return to the exercise you just did, where you reflected on your friends and identified which of them are result- oriented and which are more laid-back. The former is often referred to as Type A, while the latter is referred to as Type B. This is just one example of type.

Carl Jung, who identified the functions of how we perceive (sensing and intuition) and how we judge (thinking and feeling), also looked at these psychological aspects in relationship to introversion and extroversion.

From these roots, a number of popular models have evolved, including DISC, Myers Briggs and more.

These are just a few of the many ways our differences as people are organized into models that help us understand each other.

Among the other ways of differentiating people, there are models that include our:

- Psychological attitudes (introversion versus extroversion)
- Psychological types (how we perceive and judge)
- Personality types (action-oriented versus laid-back)
- Personality traits (how anxious, open, agreeable and pragmatic people are)
- Temperaments (logical, tactical, idealistic, strategic temperaments)

- Thinking styles (analyzers, organizers, innovators, and spiritual thinkers)
- Learning styles (visual, auditory and kinesthetic learners)
- Strengths (thinkers, doers, influencers and relationship-builders)

The models are as often identified by their creator's names as they are by theory names or acronyms.

How many aspects each model is broken into is influenced by the underlying concepts as well as how to make them memorable (thirds, quadrants, fifths, and sixteenths are common), and all have their catchy titles.

Is there a 'best' model?

Perhaps--it depends on who you ask.

None of these models is inherently right or wrong; each just emphasizes different aspects of personality, providing fresh ways to think about types of people.

Rather than prescribing how you should adapt to people based on a particular type model, we'll show you how to adapt to people regardless of how they may or may not be categorized.

Tip: You may already be familiar with a personality type model. If so, pull it out and use what you already know alongside the following suggestions.

Adapting to Type

Adapting to type is really a two-part process:

- The first part is to notice the unique qualities of a person.
- The second part is to adapt your approach based on what you have observed.

The intent here is not to psychoanalyze others.

Rather, the intent is to be aware of differences, notice cues and uncover interests that will best allow you to adjust your approach to the type of person you are dealing with.

When you can adapt your approach to what people need, and what they are and are not interested in, you increase your likelihood of being heard and will make stronger connections.

In a sense, you can be a chameleon.

Adapting to What People Respond To - Exercise

Reflect on these different personality types and what will and will not interest them. If you aren't familiar with any of the types, make your best guess.

What do you think each of these 15 types of people will be interested in?

- An analytical person
- A people person
- A person who cares about values
- An ideas person
- A creative person
- A task-oriented person
- A person who cares about fun
- A person who cares about everyone getting along
- A person who cares about connecting people
- A person who cares about finances
- A person who enjoys problem-solving
- A very logical person
- A person who is a strong leader
- A person who cares about the community
- A person who gets things done

Conversely, what type of information would cause these same 15 types of people to tune out?

- An analytical person

- A people person
- A person who cares about values
- An ideas person
- A creative person
- A task-oriented person
- A person who cares about fun
- A person who cares about everyone getting along
- A person who cares about connecting people
- A person who cares about finances
- A person who enjoys problem-solving
- A very logical person
- A person who is a strong leader
- A person who cares about the community
- A person who gets things done

Here are some of the ways you can adapt your approach:

Choice of Topic

Focus on what would be of most interest to the person. You might have to guess but reading their personality type can help you avoid talking about things that would cause them to tune you out.

Word Choice

Adapt the words you use. Use technical terms when speaking to someone with a higher education level, or who you have heard using longer words in conversation. For others, stick to shorter words that get to the point. Avoid terminology unless you are amongst those of the same profession.

Vary Your Tone

It can be useful to vary your tone of voice, and the speed of your speech to what you are hearing from the other person. If someone is speaking quietly and slowly, mirror their tone. Avoid speaking fast or loudly.

Mirror Body Language

As long as it is subtle, mirroring the other person's body language can make the person more receptive to you. If you are seated at a table, and the other person is leaning forward, do the same. If the other person is leaning back, adopt a relaxed posture.

Mood Match

If the other person is laughing and smiling, by all means, do the same. If the other person is very serious, or even stern, take their cue and use moderate facial expressions. Watch for cues as the conversation wraps up: if they become more expressive when business is done, do the same.

Adapting to What People Respond To - Possibilities

Earlier you identified what would and would not appeal to 15 different types of people. Get out your notes and compare your thoughts with the following. There are no right, and wrong answers here, just pay attention to themes.

An analytical person:

- Will be interested in details
- Will tune out if you talk about emotions

A people person:

- Will be interested in how people feel
- Will tune out if you talk about minute details

A person who cares about values:

- Will be interested in hearing about the meaning of things
- Will tune out if you talk about facts

An ideas person:

- Will be interested in hearing about possibilities
- Will tune out if you talk about timelines

A creative person:

- Will be interested in hearing about how something was created
- Will tune out if you talk about what people think about something

A task-oriented person:

- Will be interested in hearing about goals and timelines
- Will tune out if you talk about how you will gather feedback

A person who cares about fun:

- Will be interested in hearing about how accomplishments will be celebrated
- Will tune out if you talk about quality control

A person who cares about everyone getting along:

- Will be interested in hearing about how people collaborate
- Will tune out if you talk about market research

A person who cares about connecting people:

- Will be interested in hearing about who is involved
- Will tune out if you talk about milestones and deadlines

A person who cares about finances:

- Will be interested in hearing about budgets and contingency plans
- Will tune out if you talk about how you gathered feedback

A person who enjoys problem-solving:

- Will be interested in hearing about SWOT analysis (Strengths, Weaknesses, Opportunities, Threats)
- Will tune out if you talk about implementation plans

A very logical person:

- Will be interested in hearing about detailed implementation plans
- Will tune out if you talk about who came up with an idea

A person who is a strong leader:

- Will be interested in hearing about key messages
- Will tune out if you talk about project plans

A person who cares about the community:

- Will be interested in hearing about involving community members
- Will tune out if you talk about research archives

A person who gets things done:

- Will be interested in hearing about project milestones
- Will tune out if you talk about who came up with the plan

While you can never know for sure, if you pay attention to what type of person you are dealing with–or your best guess–you should be able to avoid topics that cause the person to lose interest.

If you notice that someone is tuning out (breaking eye contact, looking around, bored expression), try focusing on another aspect of the matter you are discussing or better yet, change the topic. This would be a good time to ask an open question that would invite the other person to talk about a topic of interest.

The Proposal – Possible Adaptations

Let's return to Irene, Randy, James, and Marjorie. Pull out your notes on how you might adapt your approach with each as you seek approval for your hypothetical proposal.

Did any additional ideas come to you as you read this chapter? If so, take a moment to jot them down.

When you are ready, here are some possible approaches to consider:

Irene in Purchasing:

- Needs: Measurements, financial detail, time for analysis.
- Has little time for: Lengthy explanations.
- Key to getting her approval: Be brief.
- Suggestions: Request two meetings with Irene, both short. Plan to review your proposal during the first one and return for questions and approval in a second meeting, if required. Bring an extra copy of the executive summary, measurements page, and financial details to the meeting.
- Greeting tip: Prepare a greeting that communicates how much you value her limited time, "Thanks for seeing me, Irene. I'm hoping you can help me by reviewing the measurements and financials in my training proposal. It's ready for sign-off..."
- Conversation tip: Make a comment that validates both her limited time and attention to detail, such as, "I've scheduled a second meeting next week, if needed, in case you'd like more time to analyze the details than we have today..."

Randy in Sales:

- Needs: Impacts on his sales team, how much training time will be needed.
- Has little time for: Fluff.
- Key to getting his approval: Make it easy for him to quickly grasp the program, the benefits, and what you need from him.
- Suggestions: Bring an extra copy of the executive summary to your meeting, state what you need at the beginning of the meeting. Be ready to get in and get out quickly, if needed.
- Greeting tip: Prepare a greeting that communicates that you respect his limited time, such as, "Good morning Randy. Today I am seeking your approval on the rebranding training proposal. It shouldn't take more than 5 minutes. Here is the summary..."

- Conversation tips: Be ready to give a 30-60 second summary such as, "There are three parts to the program, all of which support the rebranding strategy. The cost is $10K. Unless you have concerns about delivery, your approval today will mean completion this quarter."

James in Human Resources:

- Needs: Impacts on the people.
- Has little time for: Extraneous financial details.
- Key to getting his approval: A complete proposal with all bases covered.
- Suggestions: Prepare a couple of stories about what the lack of the program is causing. Bring an extra copy of the executive summary, just in case.
- Greeting tip: Prepare a greeting that sets the stage for his interests, such as, "Hi James. I'm excited to talk with you today about how the new rebranding training will benefit our employees…"
- Conversation tips: Prepare a few open questions that will allow him to identify the impacts, such as, "How do you see this program benefiting our employees?" or "What do you see as the biggest win from this program?"

Marjorie in Quality Management:

- Needs: How the program integrates with existing programs.
- Has little time for: Details on the reasons behind the program.
- Key to getting her approval: How easily the program can be integrated with the quality management system.
- Suggestions: Bring an extra copy of the executive summary and enlarged copies of the 3 charts. Use a highlighter to show where the program would integrate with the quality program.
- Greeting tip: Prepare a greeting that validates her interests, such as, "Hi Marjorie, I've been looking forward to this

meeting. I think I have all the ways the new training rebranding will integrate with the quality system but need your input…"

• Conversation tips: Prepare open questions, such as, "How well do you think this program integrates with the quality program? Do you see any gaps?"

• Bonus tip: Prepare a question that will secure her support, such as, "It would mean a lot if you would champion this program. It wouldn't take a lot of time but having your name behind it would help smooth implementation."

While there is no definitive right or wrong way to handle these situations, hopefully, these examples will help you see the range of possibilities.

As we wrap up this chapter, here are a few helpful caveats to keep in mind:

• Pay attention to the cues people give about their personality type and communication style.

• Adapt your approach to the person you are communicating with to help you connect and get your message across.

• If someone is in a heightened emotional state, it may not be the best time to try to engage them in conversation.

• Be sensitive to possible cultural differences.

• Don't forget that gender differences could be at play.

Tip: If you find you are interested in learning more about personality types, do an internet search as a starting point. You will find a world of resources that will allow you to dig deeper if you wish.

What do you think? Do you recognize different types in your workplace or your personal life? How can you adapt your approach to be more effective when dealing with different types of people?

Case Studies

- By adapting to type, Rebecca learned to be more concise. This in turn helped her to communicate more clearly with those who needed specific details. This was especially helpful with Anthony in accounting, as he was always asking for details without the fluff.

- Larry learned a new respect for his boss, Ernie. As he liked to involve everyone, wanted everyone to see the big picture, Ernie needed a lot of time to do this. Larry became more patient, no longer just focused on important details, and learned a few things too.

- Chris learned to adapt to what her boss, Ingrid, needed by getting to the point, not being put off by her demands. She realized that Ingrid wasn't disinterested in Chris' view, but she just needed the highlights pulled out.

- Kelly found the practice of thinking about who he would be dealing with and adapting to their style helped him get results. He found this particularly helpful in responding to people who tended to share their feelings and adapting to internal thinkers.

The Introvert's Survival Guide to Adapting to Type

Adapting your approach to what people need and what they are and are not interested in will increase your likelihood of being heard and will make stronger connections. In a word, be a chameleon.

Here are a few do's and don'ts to keep in mind:

Do's

DO adapt your approach to different types of people.

DO adapt your choice words to the person.

DO mirror the other person's body language.

DO match the other person's mood.

DO vary your tone to match the other person.

Don'ts

DON'T try to psychoanalyze others.

DON'T talk about things that will cause the other person to tune out.

DON'T overdo it with mirroring.

3 Keys to Remember

KEY 1: Be a chameleon.

KEY 2: Choose a topic of interest to the other person.

KEY 3: Avoid topics that will cause the other person to tune out.

Chapter 8: Meeting Strangers

"Strangers are only strangers until you meet them. Then they are new friends."

Unknown.

Being Approachable

Before you can meet people, you need to be approachable.

If you don't signal that you are interested in someone, they won't know. For this reason, don't just wait for someone to approach you.

Begin by outwardly demonstrating that you are open and interested in meeting people.

Instead of burying your head in your phone, adopt an open body stance, put a smile on your face and look around the room.

Stand somewhere where people are sure to walk by (near the bar always works). Simply saying hello to more people makes you more approachable.

Conversation Openers

Have a simple opening line, such as "Hello, how are you?"

Compliments always work. "What a great bag you have. Where did you get it?"

Look out for similarities and highlight these. If you see someone drinking the same type of beer, there's an opener.

As you are chatting with someone or a group of people, and someone mentions they like or dislike something you feel the same about, highlight the similarity. For example, "I know! I am so addicted to that show, too!"

If you want to talk to someone, don't overthink it. Just smile, make eye contact and say hello.

Conversation Tips

A few more tips when meeting people for the first time:

- Use your hands. Not only is this expressive, but showing your hands is considered more trustworthy.
- When you make eye contact, gaze deeply enough into the other person's eyes to notice their eye color. Just for a moment though, as you don't want to be perceived as creepy!
- Embrace your imperfections–it makes you relatable.
- It's ok to use self-deprecating humor, just don't go overboard.
- Asking 'why' is a great way to keep the conversation going.
- Say, "That reminds me of..." as a way to steer the conversation in a new direction.

- You can repeat back the last few words a person said, mirroring them, to encourage them to say more.
- Avoid using slang.

- Look for conversation sparks–if you see a person raise an eyebrow, that's a sign that they are interested in what you just said.

Chatting in Clusters

Depending on where you are, you may find yourself conversing in small clusters of people.

If you are joining a cluster, ask a question, or build a bridge. "How do you all know each other?" works well.

When you are introducing someone, a little gushing is ok, "This is Mary, and she is the most amazing Project Manager I have ever had!"

Tip: If you see two people in conversation, and their feet are pivoted in, this is a cue that they are engaged in a conversation that they don't want interrupted. This is a natural stance.

If you are chatting with someone, and you are open to others joining the conversation, consciously pivot your feet outwards. This will signal others that you are approachable.

Ending a Conversation

If you are having a great conversation, by all means, continue.

But if you are ready to move on, it's handy to have a strategy to wrap up a conversation.

You can do this by asking a question about future plans, such as what the person is doing later, this weekend, or on their vacation.

This creates the opportunity for you to make a graceful exit, such as, "It was great meeting you today. Best of luck during your upcoming move."

50 Conversation Starters

Sometimes all you need is a good question to get someone talking.

Browse the list below and pick out half a dozen questions that you could picture yourself asking. Next, rewrite them into your own words – and turn any closed questions into open questions.

1. How do you unwind from work?
2. What is your favorite pastime?
3. What are your hobbies?
4. What's your secret to stress relief?
5. What are you are you obsessed about?
6. Who is your favorite band? Why?
7. Who is your favorite singer? Why?
8. Who is your favorite singer-songwriter? Why?
9. Who is your favorite comedian? Why?
10. Who is your favorite actor? Why?
11. Who is your favorite actress? Why?
12. If something breaks, do you try to fix it, or do you just get a new one?
13. Tell me about your pets.
14. What's the best thing about your job?
15. What do you like most about your boss?
16. What subject did you like best in school?
17. Where did you go to university? What did you study?
18. What was your hobby as a child?
19. How would you describe yourself in a nutshell?
20. What is your favorite gadget?
21. What technology changed your life?
22. What do you still have and use that is really old?
23. If you were to put your name on a business, what kind of business would it be?
24. What would your motto for your business be?
25. What is your personal motto?

26. Where would you put yourself on the organized/disorganized scale?

27. What do you do to get yourself organized? How do you stay organized?

28. Do you still keep a paper calendar, or are you strictly online? Or a blend?

29. Have you ever done public speaking? What was the biggest audience? What was your topic?

30. Have you ever sung in public? What was your largest audience?

31. Have you ever done stand-up comedy? What was it like?

32. Who influenced your life the most?

33. Who did you randomly meet in your life who ended up being very important in some way?

34. What was the strangest coincidence in your life?

35. Have you experienced déjà vu?

36. What triggers your memories?

37. What is your comfort food?

38. Do you often run into people you know? Or not? Do you ever wonder about that?

39. How much sleep do you need? How much do you get?

40. Do you like napping? Why?

41. Do you ever stay up all night?

42. What is your favorite time of the year?

43. Do you like spring or fall better? Summer or winter?

44. What can't you live without?

45. What was the worst airport layover you ever experienced?

46. What was the best airport layover you ever had?

47. Where do you like to sit on a plane?

48. What do you always carry when traveling?

49. Do you experience jet lag? If not, what's your secret?

50. What kind of stuff gets on your nerves?

As we wrap up this chapter, here are a few helpful caveats to keep in mind:

- Remember that the other people you are meeting might be a bit nervous too.
- Always be ready with an open question or two.
- Have a game plan going in.

What do you think? Are you feeling a bit more comfortable about meeting strangers? Can you see how these techniques will help you be more at ease when meeting new people? What are the three or four things you will do differently?

Case Studies

- Rebecca found the strategies for meeting strangers helped her get over her anxiety by having a place to start. Now confident that she would have something to say and something interesting to ask, meant that she forgets about herself and just get curious about who she will meet.
- Larry quickly found he was meeting more people at events simply by using the conversation starters. He was even having fun, trying out the different starters, to see which worked best for him.
- Chris learned how not to be totally intimidated when meeting strangers. It was still a stretch, but the two conversation starters she memorized saved the day more than once.
- Kelly had always been pretty good at meeting people but found the conversation starters gave him new ways to steer things in a different direction.

The Introvert's Survival Guide to Meeting Strangers

You are equipped with all you need to meet strangers.

Here are a few do's and don'ts to keep in mind:

Do's

DO signal that you are approachable.

DO look for similarities.

DO be generous with compliments.

Don'ts

DON'T try to talk to two people chatting if their feet are pivoted towards each other.

DON'T try to be perfect.

DON'T hide your hands.

3 Keys to Remember

KEY 1: Be approachable.

KEY 2: Build bridges.

KEY 3: Be authentic.

Chapter 9: Getting People to Talk

Before we get started, take a blank page in your notebook and write the following. It will be used for a 2-part exercise.

Tip: You may want lots of room to write, so spread this over a few pages if you prefer.

ONE.

1:

2:

3:

TWO.

1:

2:

3:

Continue in this manner until you have room for 13 items in your notebook, like this:

THIRTEEN.

1:

2:

3:

What Would Get You to Talk? – Exercise Part 1

What are a dozen things about you that, if you were asked the right question, would give you a lot to talk about?

Hint: think about places you have traveled, famous people you have met, unusual hobbies, unique accomplishments (have you written a book? Do you have a blog? Did you once lose something important? Have a strange coincidence? Have one of the most memorable experiences in your life because of a fluke? Have an artist that you follow? Have a kitchen disaster story? Been stranded somewhere? Think, think, think…!).

In your notebook, pull out the worksheet you just created and jot a note about each story next to the numbers in capitals (ONE, TWO, THREE….), like this:

ONE. ← Put your first story here

1:

2:

3:

TWO. ← Put your second story here

1:

2:

3:

And so on. Yes, there is even room for 13 stories on your worksheet, in case you think of one more and want to make it a baker's dozen!

You don't need to write out each story in any detail–just a few words to jog your memory will suffice.

What Would Get You to Talk? – Exercise Part 2

Now, return to your list. What are a couple of questions that someone could ask that would cause you to bring up each of your stories in response?

Just in case you are wondering what the point is, this exercise is designed to help you craft conversation starters of your own that just might turn up magic with the people you meet. Play along... it can only benefit you!

YOUR STORY ONE.

1: ← Put your first question here

2: ← Put your second question here

3: ← Put your third question here

And so on.

Your goal is to come up with 2-3 questions per story.

Getting Other People to Talk

Remember that people love to talk about themselves, so if you have a warm and friendly greeting and ask open questions, you will find yourself engaged in conversation.

Don't forget that mastering open questions is your SECRET KEY t0 getting people to talk with you.

When you ask people questions about themselves and are genuinely curious, they will want to share with you.

Don't forget about nodding your head. As introduced earlier, a 'triple nod' when someone stops speaking will signal that you are waiting for them to continue.

Your Magic Conversation Starters

Refer back to the stories you identified about yourself and the questions you came up with that would draw them out of you.

From your list, pick 3-5 questions that you think would be particularly helpful in getting other people to talk about their experiences.

Write these on a fresh page, so that they are easy to find and read for future reference.

1.

2.

3.

4.

5.

Next time you are going to an event, review your Magic Conversation Starters and pick one or two you plan to use.

Tip: print your Magic Conversation Starters out and slip them into your wallet – or take a picture with your Smartphone.

Bonus: 100 More Conversation Starters

Have fun looking over this list of 100 more conversation starters. It's important to make them 'yours,' so adapt these to your interests and jot down others that come to you.

Tip: watch for closed questions below and challenge yourself to rewrite them into open questions that sound natural for you.

1. What's a trend you miss?
2. What surprising thing do you keep in your wallet or purse?
3. What famous person have you met? Tell me the story.
4. What famous person do you wish you'd met?
5. What famous person did you almost meet?
6. Have you ever experienced something you can't explain?
7. How do you get yourself out of a funk?
8. Do you prefer time with others or time alone?
9. Do you pack light or take as much as you can?
10. Do you like beach vacations? Why?
11. How many books are by your bed? What are they?
12. Do you carry reading material with you?
13. You are 10 minutes early to a meeting. How do you spend your time?
14. What is a charity you have been involved with?
15. What product was discontinued that you wish they'd bring back?

16. What invention do you wish you'd come up with?

17. What kind of thing lifts your spirits? Why?

18. What movie surprised you? Why?

19. What was the worst movie you ever saw? Why?

20. What was the best movie you ever saw? Why?

21. What documentary do you recommend?

22. What is your special talent?

23. What is your greatest indulgence?

24. Have you ever been stuck in an elevator?

25. Do you take transit? How do you like it?

26. What's your strangest transit story?

27. Do you buy lottery tickets? Have you ever won?

28. Do you still have cable TV?

29. Do you still have a landline? Why?

30. What's the best gift anyone ever gave you?

31. What's the gift you were most excited to give?

32. Do you like to plan ahead when you travel, or do you prefer to just let things unfold?

33. Do you drive a standard or an automatic? If both, which do you prefer?

34. Do you have a car? Do you own it or lease it?

35. What was your favorite car?

36. What was your first car?

37. Have you ever participated in any kind of car co-op or other car sharing service?

38. In your experience, what was the best cartoon ever made?

39. Are you a reader? What's your favorite genre?

40. What are you reading right now?

41. Do you prefer to read 'real' physical books over other formats??

42. Have you ever read an eBook? What do you like about eBooks?

43. Do you listen to audiobooks? Do you enjoy them the same or differently from physical books?

44. If you read physical books, do you buy them new? Used? Or do you get them from the library?

45. You have an hour free. There is a coffee shop and a library? Which do you gravitate towards?

46. How many books do you read a week/month/year?

47. What's the best book you've read in the past year?

48. Did you have your own room as a child, or did you share?

49. Have you ever lived alone? What's the longest you've lived alone?

50. What news stories are you watching these days?

51. What was the most interesting trip you've ever taken?

52. Do you do any art? Do you paint or draw?

53. Are you an art fan? Who are your favorite artists?

54. Do you visit art galleries and museums when you travel?

55. What's the best museum you have ever visited?

56. Have you ever been to New York? When and what did you like about it?

57. Do you like Broadway-style shows? What's the best one you've ever seen?

58. Do you ever go to plays? What's the most memorable play you ever saw?

59. Have you ever done any acting? What about in school?

60. Do you ever find yourself quoting Seinfeld?

61. Do you have a favorite movie you like to re-watch every once in a while?

62. Are you a person who answers your cell phone all the time? Or do you just use it for outgoing calls?

63. Have you ever cruised? What did you like about it?

64. What's the best beach you have ever been to?

65. Have you ever been to a professional sports game?

66. Have you ever been to the Olympics? What was the experience like?

67. Do you watch the Olympics? Which do you prefer: The Summer Olympics or Winter Olympics?

68. Do you follow the Paralympics?

69. Have you ever been to Expo? If so, what year?

70. Who inspires you?

71. Do you ever go "off grid"?

72. What do you prefer, baths or showers?

73. Coke or Pepsi?

74. What type of hotel do you like to stay in?

75. When you travel, do you prefer a small town or a big city?

76. When you travel, do you plan ahead for the restaurants you are going to dine at? Or do you just taking things as they go?

77. What do you like most about large cities?

78. What do you like least about large cities?

79. Have you ever planned a trip just to see an exhibit at a museum? Tell me about it.

80. Have you ever planned a trip just to see a play or theatre production? What was it?

81. Have you ever planned a trip just to go to a concert? What was that like?

82. Would you ever plan a trip just to see a sporting event?

83. Do you run marathons?

84. Have you ever planned a trip around a marathon or other event you have competed in?

85. Have you ever attended an international conference? Where was it? What was particularly interesting about it?

86. Hawaiian pizza. Yes or no?

87. Do you have a favorite charity that you support?

88. What's the most embarrassing thing that has ever happened to you?

89. Are you a practical joker? Do you play pranks? What's the best prank you ever pulled off?

90. What's the best practical joke anyone has ever played on you?

91. Have you ever been fooled on April Fool's Day?

92. Have you ever fooled someone else on April Fool's Day?

93. What professional associations do you belong to?

94. What are your career aspirations?

95. What are your retirement plans?

96. Do you prefer to start your day with tea or coffee?

97. Have you ever taken an online course? What was it, and what was it like?

98. Is your primary computer a PC or a Mac?

99. Do you have GPS in your car?

100. Have you ever lost your car in a parking lot?

As we wrap up this chapter, here are a few helpful caveats to keep in mind:

- Remember that great questions are the key to getting people to talk.
- Try the triple nod to keep them talking!

What do you think? Do you see how human nature works when you ask people to talk about themselves? Are you inspired to try?

Case Studies

- Rebecca noticed a big improvement once she started asking people more about themselves. No longer were things lapsing into silence when conversation ran out upon meeting someone new.
- Larry began enjoying his new abilities to have more enriching discussions at networking events.
- Chris learned ways to get others to talk more and take the focus off herself. She'd met some pretty interesting people, too.
- Kelly honed his skills to get more out of business interactions.
-

The Introvert's Survival Guide to Getting People to Talk

Be ready to get the people you meet to talk with you by planning ahead.

Here are a few do's and don'ts to keep in mind:

Do's

DO ask open questions

DO prepare questions that will entice people to open up.

DO ask questions designed to have people share their stories.

DO use the triple nod.

Don'ts

DON'T ask a question that is commonly asked.

DON'T ask closed questions.

3 Keys to Remember

KEY 1: Have your Magic Conversation Starter questions ready.

KEY 2: Adopt your open body stance.

KEY 3: Listen actively.

Chapter 10: Increasing Your Likability

"The deepest urge in human nature is the desire to be important."

John Dewey

The Desire to Be Important - Exercise

We began this chapter with a quote from John Dewey, the American psychologist and philosopher:

Take a few minutes to contemplate Dewey's words, and ask yourself how you can use this sentiment to succeed in conversation.

Make a few notes, and we'll return to this later in the chapter.

The Charisma Myth

Forget Hollywood and what you thought you learned about charisma. The most charismatic people *aren't* the ones that go on and on about themselves. So don't be a conversational narcissist!

People really aren't that interested in hearing you talk about yourself. What they are most interested in is talking about themselves!

Being Likeable

The most important thing is to think about how you can get the other person to talk.

It should go without saying, but don't insult the other person and don't act creepy (avoid personal questions and staring).

Don't make yourself superior. Don't boast. Don't brag. Better yet, don't talk about yourself.

Finally, don't gossip, speak ill of others or 'overhead gaze' to see who might be more interesting to talk to (!).

The Desire to Be Important - Possibilities

"The deepest urge in human nature is the desire to be important."

John Dewey

Earlier in the chapter, you reflected on the above quote from John Dewey, and how this sentiment can be used to succeed in conversation.

Perhaps you thought of the following:

> • If you ask someone about themselves, they may open up to you.
>
> • If you express a genuine interest in someone, they may share their unique story with you.
>
> • If you continue to demonstrate your interest, by your body language and follow-up questions, they will feel the glow of importance that Dewey is referring to.
>
> • When you are interested in another in this way, they will like you.
>
> • Therefore, asking people about themselves in conversation, is the key to likeability.

As we wrap up this chapter, here are a few helpful caveats to keep in mind:

- It's always better to be the one asking the questions.
- To genuinely demonstrate interest in another person, use your body language, eye contact, and follow-up questions.
- Like yourself–people are far more likely to like someone who likes themselves and has high self-esteem.

What do you think? What do you think about the impact of likeability on your interactions? Do you think you can increase your likeability? How can you do so while staying true to yourself?

Case Studies

- A bit ambivalent, as she wasn't that worried whether people liked her or not, Rebecca came around when she realized likeability would help her improve her communications and results.
- Larry had never thought about likeability before. Eyes opened, he found he liked analyzing other's likability.
- Chris learned she was more likable than she thought.
- Kelly thought this was mostly a lark, but then realized he responded differently to those that presented as likable.

The Introvert's Survival Guide to Likeability

Now that we've crushed the Hollywood myth about charisma and identified that the thing people are most interested in talking about is themselves, the door is open for you to increase your likeability.

Here are a few do's and don'ts to keep in mind:

Do's

DO express a genuine interest in others.

DO ask a question that invites someone to share their story with you.

Don'ts

DON'T be a conversational narcissist!

DON'T gossip.

DON'T speak ill of others.

DON'T 'overhead gaze' to find someone more interesting to talk to.

DON'T forget: you can't please everybody.

3 Keys to Remember

KEY 1: If you make a person feel important, they will like you.

KEY 2: We like people who like us.

KEY 3: Be authentic.

Chapter 11: Finding Your Voice

This chapter will explore finding your voice on three different fronts:

- Literally, in terms of voice tone, volume, speed, inflection, and so on.
- Metaphorically, as in the confidence to speak with authenticity.
- In the power of storytelling.

As these are broad topics and the latter two beyond the scope of this book, these are mainly starting points for you to begin your own exploration.

Tone of Voice

As was introduced in Chapter 6: Non-Verbal Communication, a speaker's tone of voice can have a huge impact on the message the listener hears.

As you will recall, messages are conveyed by:

- The words spoken: 10%
- Tone of voice: 40%
- Body language: 50%

So, roughly 40% of a message is conveyed by the speaker's tone of voice.

A voice tone that is loud, quiet, stern, cheerful, low, high, fast or slow will affect what the listener hears from the speaker.

The News of the Day – Exercise

Refer to today's news. If you have a newspaper, great. If not, go online to find a news story of interest to you. Pick a story that isn't overly negative or positive. Perhaps a human-interest story or a play review.

Once you have picked out a story, read it aloud eight (8) times, and observe how your tone changes the message.

Tip: if you have someone at home or at work that can do this exercise with you, you will find it more enlightening. Even a friend can do it over the phone with you.

Make notes about what different meaning you noticed when you read the story:

Loudly

Softly/quietly

Sternly

Cheerfully

With a low voice tone

With a high voice tone

Quickly

Slowly

The Full Range - Exercise

What do you think these variations in voice may mean?

Talking fast

Talking slowly

Talking loudly

Talking quietly

Yelling

Screaming

Whispering

Fluctuating voice volume

Fading out

Stuttering

Speaking haltingly

Singing

Speaking emphatically (stressing words)

Mumbling

Using a harsh tone of voice

Using an accusing tone of voice

Using a gentle tone of voice

Using a friendly tone of voice

Using an unfriendly tone of voice

Using a sarcastic tone of voice

As these are open to interpretation, and so much varies based on the message, the speaker and the listener, there are no definitive answers. The purpose here is to be aware of the very many ways a message can be altered by the way in which it is spoken.

Metaphorically Speaking

In literature, you will find many references to when one 'finds one's own voice'.

This typically refers to when someone advances in their own personal development to have confidence in what they believe and are at a place where they can speak with authenticity about these beliefs. When these come together, we say that a person has found their voice.

Finding Your Voice - Exercise

Where are you on the journey of finding your voice? How confident are you in your beliefs? When you speak about these things, do you find yourself speaking with authenticity? Or do you still have a way to go on this journey? You may find that you have found your voice in one aspect of your life, but not in another.

Set aside some time to journal about these questions.

Tip: You may find that you return to the theme of finding your voice over time as your beliefs evolve.

Storytelling

You only need to look around yourself virtually to find references to stories and storytelling today. It is like the old art of the storyteller has been resurrected in modern times.

You'll find deep examples of storytelling in memoirs, blogs, podcasts and in your community.

You'll find less deep, but not necessarily less meaningful, examples of storytelling in your social media feed.

Regardless of format, chances are that introverts are behind many or most of these stories, as introverts are our writers and those who connect the dots for the rest of us.

Storytelling in Your Life – Exercise

Pick one of the storytelling methods listed above to explore or another of your choosing.

Spend some time reading and listening to the stories you encounter.

As you do, reflect on how you can bring storytelling into your life, either to learn more about others or to share your story.

Enjoy the journey.

As we wrap up this chapter, here are a few helpful caveats to keep in mind:

- Voice can mean different things to different people in different contexts.
- If you are interested in learning more about voice tone in particular, you may find YouTube videos a great resource, as you can actually hear the speaker.

What do you think? Does your voice impact the message you send? Do you need to work with your voice to come across more effectively? How? Do you need to talk louder, softer, with more inflection? How can you apply these skills when telling stories?

Case Studies

- Rebecca truly found her voice and learned how to influence process so that there was an opportunity to contribute her ideas. This relieved huge stress, and she found herself being more open to others and their ideas.
- Larry never really thought he needed to 'find his voice' but had in fact made big strides at networking events, big and small. He became much more comfortable in larger groups.
- This was a huge growth area for Chris, as she found ways to ensure she was heard and got the satisfaction of having her input taken seriously. Chris was quickly able to see a major positive change at work as a result of her input.
- Having already found his voice, Kelly used the tips to hone his storytelling skills.

Chapter 12: Networking 101

Natalie and Nettie went to a silent auction together. As they both were introverts and were trying to get better about these things, they decided to split up so they could meet different people.

Natalie, "It was ok, but the small talk kills me. I was so bored."

Nettie, "Really? I had a blast. But then again, I'm a rebel. One guy asked me a question about the weather, so I pretended he asked me about the last time I lost my car in a parking lot, which was last week, and I answered that instead. Turns out he's done it twice. We had a good chuckle, then had a good conversation about cars."

A good place to start our discussion on networking is to think about your friends and colleagues that you have seen in networking situations. What are your observations? Do they seem to be enjoying themselves? Are they meeting new people? Or are they just hanging out with the usual gang?

Now think about strangers you have observed at events, apparently networking with ease. What specifically have you noticed about these people? What makes you think they are at ease?

It is easy to assume that everyone else at a networking event is having an easy time but comfort yourself with the knowledge that you have no idea who else is faking it.

Wallflowers, Minglers, and Aces

It can be helpful to divide those at networking events into three rough categories:

Wallflowers

If you are reading this book, you probably don't need much of an explanation of the Wallflowers.

Minglers

These are those people who are managing in the middle, and it's not a bad place to be. For the most part, Minglers are able to calmly arrive at an event, introduce themselves to others with relative ease, and move in and out of conversations as the need arises. This is your goal.

Aces

These are the networking Aces that you imagine floating through the event with ease, knowing everyone, or breezily introducing themselves to anyone new. Things aren't always what they seem, and these folks can make plenty of networking mistakes (such as dominating the conversation, forgetting to share contact details or having too much to drink). But this is not your goal.

You don't need to 'ace' networking events. You just need to calm your inner butterflies and get them to fly in formation. And, yes, it is possible to transform yourself from a Wallflower to a Mingler.

Networking Skills Self-Assessment

Take a few minutes to reflect on your networking skills.

1. You are going to an event with networking opportunities. Do you:

a) Turn up and see what happens?

b) Have a goal or two in mind?

c) Develop a networking strategy?

2 . As you hang up your jacket, there are 3-4 others doing the same. Do you:

a) Keep to yourself

b) Start an informal conversation about the weather

c) Introduce yourself

3. A waiter comes by with a tray of champagne glasses. Do you:

a) Accept one, hoping you won't get tipsy on an empty stomach

b) Accept one, grateful for the snack you had at home

c) Accept one and take another 'for a friend'

4. You and one other person are at the dessert table. Do you:

a) Continue to quietly study the desserts

b) Start a conversation

c) Suggest the two of you conduct a taste test

6. You are standing alone at an event. Do you:

a) Wait for someone to approach you?

b) Join a conversation nearby?

c) Wouldn't happen, why would I be standing alone?

7. You see someone standing alone at an event. Do you:

a) Commiserate but stay put?

b) Go over and introduce yourself?

c) Nothing. You are too busy to notice someone standing on the sidelines.

8. There is a group of people chatting and laughing. Do you:

a) Stay away?

b) Wander over and gently join in?

c) Happily join in, adding to the joke or just say, "You all sound like fun!"

9. The event is over, and you are on your way home. What's in your pocket?

a) A napkin and a couple toothpicks

b) A few of business cards

c) A big bunch of business cards

10. It is the day after the networking event. What do you do?

a) Nothing, other than feel grateful that you survived it.

b) Pull out the business cards, making notes and a follow-up plan.

c) Add the names to your contacts and set up a lunch date.

If you mostly answered the first option (a), then you are probably a Wallflower. Don't worry, there's lots of opportunities to transition to a Mingler.

If you mostly answered the second option (b), then you are probably a Mingler. If you answered some a's, then keep working at it. Otherwise, you are in a great spot. When you're feeling brave, you can take things to the next level.

If you mostly answered the third option (c), then you are probably an Ace. That can be a good thing, mostly, but make sure you aren't going overboard. You still need a strategy. And remember it's more important to build your network than to be the life of the party.

Networking for Introverts

Networking is much touted, but there is a bias towards extroversion in this context.

With that in mind, here are a few networking tips, specific to introverts:

- Remember that networking books and tips are geared towards extroverts.
- Reframe networking so it works for you.
- Find someone you can connect with.
- As you look around the room, ask yourself, "Where's one person I can have a great conversation with?"
- Look for kindred spirits.
- Once you've met that one person, it's ok if you want to stop there.
- Take the pressure off yourself to perform or network like the extroverts.

Keep these tips in mind as you read the rest of this chapter.

Most importantly, remember that you have permission to reframe networking so it works for you. There is no one right way to do this!

Mastering Small Talk

Does anyone ever really master small talk? Maybe. Maybe not. But here are a few hints, nonetheless.

- Remember that the banter that we call small talk is really just filler until you can land on something interesting to talk about.
- If someone asks you a closed question, pretend they asked you an open question and answer that instead. For example, if you are asked, "Did you like this morning's speaker?" respond by sharing a comment about something the speaker said that you particularly liked.

- Answer a more interesting question than the one you were asked. For example, if you are asked what you are planning to do next weekend, answer by sharing a story about the amazing vacation you have planned for next month. Or, if you are asked if you think the wind will pick up, answer instead by telling them about what happened to your house during last week's windstorm.

- When you are telling a story, pause to create spots where others can jump in. Or create an opening by saying, "Has anyone else ever had this happen to them?!?"

- Have a mini-poll in your mind and ask everyone you meet for their opinion. Just say, "Oh, I'm asking everyone what their favorite coffee spot is. Can you tell me yours? And why?"

- Don't forget about nodding your head. As introduced earlier, a 'triple nod' when someone stops speaking acts as a signal that you are waiting for them to continue.

- Don't sweat it–have your Magic Conversation Starters ready to go and you may never get stuck in small talk again!

The Transformation from Wallflower to Mingler

Here are a few guidelines to help you transform yourself from a Wallflower to a Mingler:

- Plan to arrive early to get the lay of the land.
- Set a goal of how many people you want to meet.
- Initiate conversations versus waiting to be approached.
- Say your name with confidence.
- Have your elevator pitch ready (who you are and what you do, in 15 seconds).
- Have your conversation starter picked out.
- Share contact information.
- Leave a hand free for shaking (don't get burdened by wine, a plate of nibbles and a napkin).

- Have a snack before you go.
- Limit yourself to one drink–or stick to soda.

As you build your skills, here are 5 extra tips for 'the brave':

- Introduce yourself to someone you see standing alone.
- Leave the perimeter of the room.
- Join a cluster of people already talking (it's ok, try it; if you can't break in, just move on).
- Introduce yourself to someone you've always wanted to meet (guest speaker, industry leader).
- If you see someone you've met before, but can't remember their name, approach them and re-introduce yourself.

Here are a few bonus tips:

- Stick to events where there is a focus, such as a speaker, and avoid events that are strictly networking (unless you have a small business and are seeking leads, you're unlikely to have deep conversations at these).
- If you're comfortable, wear something that invariably brings compliments or starts conversations. This makes it easy for someone to approach you.
- Think about how you can help others make connections. For example, if you meet someone who is embarking on self-publishing their first book, and you know someone who has just done this, offer to connect them. This *is* networking!

Although they will take practice, hopefully you can now envision some of the things you can do to begin networking with increasing ease.

To get the most out of networking, however, you need a broader strategy.

3-Part Networking Strategy

No matter what type of event you will be attending, employ this three-part networking strategy to get the most out of each opportunity.

1. Have a goal

Having a question you want to be answered or something you want to learn can make the difference between randomly killing time and a satisfying outcome.

2. Take a leap

Plan to start at least one conversation or have a great conversation starter question ready if someone approaches you first.

3. Act with intention

You will be at the networking event to meet people, but unless you act with intention, you could find that you haven't really met anyone at all.

Use all you have learned to create your own 3-Part Networking Strategy for the events you attend. Review it again afterward and tweak it for the next time around.

Who knows, maybe people will be referring to you as an excellent networker in the future!

As we wrap up this chapter, here are a few helpful caveats to keep in mind:

- There is no one right way to network.
- Reinvent networking to make it work for you.
- Avoid events that are strictly for networking–look for events with an activity or speaker that are part of the agenda.
- Don't try to be an extrovert.

What do you think? Do you envision feeling more comfortable at networking events by applying these skills? Are you tempted to try?

Perhaps you have been to a networking event since beginning this chapter: how did it go, what did you do differently, how did other people respond? What are your goals for your next networking event?

Case Studies

- Now that Rebecca was more comfortable sharing her ideas at work, she had a little more interest and less anxiety when it came to networking events. By honoring her need for time alone to re-energize, she found that even if she arrived late, she was in better form than if she rushed to events right after work.

- Larry had a huge boost in confidence with regards to his networking skills. Equipped with his 'story in a nutshell', a reliable set of open questions to use when meeting new people, and a few clever questions to get people he knew thinking and talking, he soon found himself networking with enthusiasm.

- Chris now felt she could survive a networking session by not clamming up if someone introduced themselves to her or asked about her life. She was thrilled to learn the 'arrive-early' approach to feel less awkward.

- Kelly already had pretty good networking skills but tried out many of the tips as he wanted to take things to the next level. He found that having a plan and acting with intention brought pretty remarkable results.

The Introvert's Survival Guide to Small Talk

While you may never love small talk, you can survive it and even enjoy it.

Here are a few do's and don'ts to keep in mind:

Do's

DO allow yourself to be interrupted.

DO create opportunities for others to jump in.

DO give interesting answers to boring questions.

DO have a mini-poll that you can use.

Don'ts

DON'T answer a boring question with a boring answer.

DON'T just stand there.

DON'T sneak a look at your phone.

DON'T fall asleep.

3 Keys to Remember

KEY 1: Pretend you were asked an interesting question and answer it.

KEY 2: Have your Magic Conversation Starter questions ready.

KEY 3: The banter is just occupying you until you land on a more interesting topic.

The Introvert's Guide to 7 Different Types of Networking Opportunities

As there are many different types of networking opportunities and call for different strategies, the following are Introvert Guides to seven common types:

- Networking Events
- Lecture-Style Presentations
- Workshops and Classes
- Luncheons
- Dinners
- Conferences
- Trade Shows

The Introvert's Guide to Networking–at Networking Events

Did you know that some events are designed solely as networking events? If you haven't encountered one yet, you may in the future. The downside is that there isn't necessarily a speaker or an activity, but the upside is that everyone has the same goal as you do--to meet as many people as possible. As others are also interested in building up their personal networks, your attempts to practice your networking skills will be celebrated.

Here are a few do's and don'ts to keep in mind:

Do's

DO take lots of business cards.

DO have your 3o-second elevator pitch ready.

DO dress comfortably.

DO wear clothes that make you feel confident.

Don'ts

DON'T just hang out at the dessert table.

DON'T just chat with people you know.

DON'T forget to ask for others' business cards.

3 Keys to Remember

KEY 1: Exude confidence.

KEY 2: Exchange contact information.

KEY 3: Follow-up with at least one person afterward.

Remember to employ the 3-Part Networking Strategy: 1. Have a goal, 2. Take a leap and 3. Act with intention.

The Introvert's Guide to Networking–at Lecture-Style Presentations

Lecture-style presentations typically have what is referred to as theatre seating, with rows of chairs, all facing forward, perhaps with an aisle or two. This format is common at conferences.

Here are a few do's and don'ts to keep in mind:

Do's

DO arrive early enough that you can get your preferred seating, especially if you need to sit in a certain spot to see or hear.

DO pick an aisle seat if you are prone to needing to get out or want an exit strategy.

DO leave your jacket or a book on your chair, then wander the room to network.

DO say hello to a couple of people and start a conversation.

DO introduce yourself to the people who end up sitting next to you.

DO think of a question you want to be answered.

Don'ts

DON'T just grab a seat and sit there reading the flyer.

DON'T just wait by looking at your Smartphone.

DON'T try to balance a coffee cup, a piece of cake, your iPad and a notepad on your lap unless you want to start a conversation with the person you spill coffee on.

DON'T be afraid to ask a question.

3 Keys to Remember

KEY 1: Arrive early.

KEY 2: Introduce yourself to your seatmates.

KEY 3: Think of a question you want to be answered.

Remember to employ the 3-Part Networking Strategy: 1. Have a goal, 2. Take a leap and 3. Act with intention.

The Introvert's Guide to Networking–at Workshops and Classes

Chances are that you have taken plenty of courses in your life, and chances are that you will take many more. Whether as stand-alone events or as part of conferences, workshops and classes are a great networking opportunity.

The two most common seating arrangements are round tables or rows of tables with chairs. Regardless of format, you want to be seated both for ideal learning and for networking.

Here are a few do's and don'ts to keep in mind:

Do's

DO arrive early.

DO introduce yourself to the instructor or workshop leader (even if you feel a bit awkward doing so, you are likely to find that you will be more relaxed once you have made this personal connection).

DO get a seat that you will be physically comfortable at.

DO be the one to pipe up and introduce yourself to the other early arrivals.

DO have a question or two in mind for the day.

Don'ts

DON'T sit with your colleagues if you aren't attending alone.

DON'T find excuses to not participate in the activities.

DON'T hide behind your phone.

3 Keys to Remember

KEY 1: Have learning goals.

KEY 2: Be open-minded to different perspectives.

KEY 3: Participate actively.

Remember to employ the 3-Part Networking Strategy: 1. Have a goal, 2. Take a leap and 3. Act with intention.

The Introvert's Guide to Networking–at Luncheons

Do you find yourself attending luncheon meetings, listening to speaker sessions held over lunch, or participating in social luncheons? With just a few strategies you can find yourself enjoying successful conversations at luncheons without giving into anxieties.

Here are a few do's and don'ts to keep in mind:

Do's

DO get a seat early so that you can see the speaker without needing to turn your chair or strain your neck.

DO ask if you can join a table with just a couple of people at it.

DO invite people to join your table.

DO have a spare pen and paper you can share.

DO have a question in mind that you want to be answered.

Don'ts

DON'T be afraid to start a new table if there is open seating and many tables.

DON'T be satisfied if the person next to you isn't talkative; turn to the person on your other side or even across the table and start a conversation.

DON'T just sit at the table looking at your Smartphone.

DON'T eat soup unless you are particularly adept at not spilling.

3 Keys to Remember

KEY 1: Get seated comfortably.

KEY 2: Plan to meet your tablemates.

KEY 3: Have a question you want to be answered.

Remember to employ the 3-Part Networking Strategy: 1. Have a goal, 2. Take a leap and 3. Act with intention.

The Introvert's Guide to Networking–at Dinners

While there are similarities between lunches and dinners, in terms of networking there are some important differences. Dinners, banquets and other sit-down affairs tend to be more elaborate affairs. Lasting longer and more formal in nature, you will spend more time with those you are seated with.

Here are a few do's and don'ts to keep in mind:

Do's

DO get a seat early.

DO start a new table at a sit-down function with many tables.

DO think of a question you want to be answered, a person you want to meet, or a personal goal for the evening.

DO carry business cards and share them.

DO look for friendly faces and ask if you can join their table.

Don'ts

DON'T wear clothes with droopy sleeves.

DON'T try to join a table with just one or two seats left, as you could very well hear that the spot is being saved.

DON'T eat food for the first time unless you have a varied palate and like most everything.

DON'T complain about the food; if something is not to your liking, just leave it aside.

DON'T reach; ask for the cream/butter/salt and pepper to be passed.

DON'T drink too much.

3 Keys to Remember

KEY 1: Get a great seat.

KEY 2: Be flexible.

KEY 3: Go easy with the wine.

Remember to employ the 3-Part Networking Strategy: 1. Have a goal, 2. Take a leap and 3. Act with intention.

The Introvert's Guide to Networking–at Conferences

Conferences offer tremendous networking opportunities. In addition to lectures, workshops, luncheons, and dinners, you will find yourself meeting other delegates during registration, between events, at mixers and other activities. It is important to set yourself up for success to get the most out of your conference time.

In addition to learning goals (the sessions you will attend) and self-care goals (healthy snacks and walks), set networking goals for yourself. A networking plan will help you leverage the best networking opportunities, avoid time- wasters that could cause you to have less time for conversation, and escape from moments of anxiety.

Note: see the next Introvert's Guide for tips specific to trade shows.

Here are a few do's and don'ts to keep in mind:

Do's

DO set goals for the conference.

DO have a question planned that you can ask of others you meet.

DO get a big picture of the conference, planning out what you want to attend, and who you want to meet.

DO have an anti-anxiety plan.

DO splurge a little and get a hotel room on-site or across the street (handy for a bit of a break; it's also handy for skipping washroom lineups).

Don'ts

DON'T attend all the same sessions if you go with a colleague.

DON'T be afraid to get up and leave a session if it is not of interest (duck into another session or take an introvert's me-break and come back restored).

DON'T spend your time between sessions engaged with your Smartphone.

3 Keys to Remember

KEY 1: Have a plan.

KEY 2: Be open and open-minded.

KEY 3: Take care of your creature comforts.

Remember to employ the 3-Part Networking Strategy: 1. Have a goal, 2. Take a leap and 3. Act with intention.

The Introvert's Guide to Networking–at Trade Shows

Trade shows, which feature vendors with booths that participants visit, are a common feature of conferences or may be stand-alone events. Trade shows are informative, however larger trade shows can be daunting, with hundreds of booths, hours of walking on concrete floors and much collecting swag and entering contests. One can leave a trade show exhausted and barely remembering who you met. For this reason, it's a good idea to have a plan.

Here are a few do's and don'ts to keep in mind:

Do's

DO carry lots of business cards.

DO study the trade show map and pick out a few booths you really want to visit.

DO start a conversation at the booths of greatest interest to you.

DO engage in conversation with other attendees.

DO set a goal, such as plan one person to follow up with afterward.

Don'ts

DON'T try to see everything.

DON'T just wander aimlessly.

DON'T get caught up in the gimmicks of collecting a trinket, stamp or contest entry at every booth.

DON'T expect yourself to go for hours without a little break for yourself.

3 Keys to Remember

KEY 1: Wear comfortable shoes.

KEY 2: Have a 3-point plan.

KEY 3: Do it your way.

Remember to employ the 3-Part Networking Strategy: 1. Have a goal, 2. Take a leap and 3. Act with intention.

Chapter 13: Special Situations

You may encounter one or more of these special one-off situations:

- Interviews
- Business Meetings
- Office Communications
- Office Parties
- Volunteering

If you do, you will find an Introvert's Guide for each at the end of this chapter.

What do you think? Do you have any special situations that aren't included in this list? If so, think about the principles in this book, brainstorm a few ideas and create your own Introvert's Guide for these situations.

Case Studies

- Rebecca had never felt comfortable at office parties, but armed with the new tips, she actually found herself recently enjoying a work-related social gathering.

- The tips helped Larry in both his business meetings and surprisingly with his family.
- Chris found herself more effective with the volunteer groups she was involved in.
- Kelly gained great perspectives in terms of office parties, where he'd never really thought about how much to drink, or how his actions impacted his reputation.

The Introvert's Guide to 5 Special Situations

As each type of special situation calls for different strategies, the following are Introvert Guides to these five special situations:

- Interviews
- Business Meetings
- Office Communications
- Office Parties
- Volunteering

The Introvert's Survival Guide to Interviews

Interviews are a unique situation. When you are applying for a job or contract, your priority is on putting your best foot forward–and proceeding to the next step in the hiring process.

Here are a few do's and don'ts to keep in mind:

Do's

DO be on time.

DO dress professionally in clothes that make you feel confident.

DO bring a spare copy of your resume.

DO use your active listening skills.

DO ask open questions.

DO have a clean notepad and pen ready.

DO use the interviewer's name.

DO smile.

Don'ts

DON'T be late.

DON'T treat the receptionist disrespectfully.

DON'T speak despairingly about your former employers.

DON'T interrupt the interviewer.

DON'T doubt yourself.

3 Keys to Remember

KEY 1: Be confident.

KEY 2: Be prepared.

KEY 3: Be professional.

The Introvert's Survival Guide to Business Meetings

Business meetings aren't all that different from some of the networking events covered in the previous chapter, except that the focus is on the business, rather than networking. That said, there are still opportunities to network.

Here are a few do's and don'ts to keep in mind:

Do's

DO be on time.

DO carry business cards.

DO introduce yourself to everyone at the meeting who you haven't met before.

DO introduce others who may not have met each other.

DO use your active listening skills.

DO ask open questions.

DO create opportunities for introverts to contribute to the discussion.

Don'ts

DON'T be invisible.

DON'T goof off.

DON'T speak despairingly about your company or the competition.

DON'T confuse the business meeting with a personal setting; stay professional.

DON'T ask closed or leading questions.

3 Keys to Remember

KEY 1: Be professional.

KEY 2: Use open questions.

KEY 3: Meet someone new.

The Introvert's Survival Guide to the Office Communications

If you work in an office, then communications with your co-workers are part of your everyday life. Whether you mostly work alone, or interact extensively with others all day long, there are common communication situations you will face.

Here are a few do's and don'ts to keep in mind:

Do's

DO be present.

DO contribute your ideas.

DO participate.

DO use your active listening skills.

DO ask great open questions.

DO pay attention to your body language.

Don'ts

DON'T badmouth your employer.

DON'T forget to leave time to recharge your batteries.

DON'T ask leading or closed questions.

3 Keys to Remember

KEY 1: Find ways to contribute your ideas.

KEY 2: Consider your needs as an introvert.

KEY 3: Stretch yourself, if and when you are ready.

The Introvert's Survival Guide to Office Parties

Office party? Sure, go. But don't let it ruin your career.

Here are a few do's and don'ts to keep in mind:

Do's

DO plan who you want to meet.

DO think about the best time to arrive.

DO dress comfortably and confidently.

DO pick a few conversation starters.

DO be a gracious guest.

Don'ts

DON'T drink a lot.

DON'T behave inappropriately.

DON'T put yourself in a situation where you will feel uncomfortable.

DON'T stay if you aren't having a good time.

3 Keys to Remember

KEY 1: Limit the booze.

KEY 2: Fly under the radar.

KEY 3: Find someone interesting to talk to.

The Introvert's Survival Guide to Volunteering

Volunteering is a great way to practice and enhance your communication skills. Plus you'll meet some great people while making a difference in your community.

Here are a few do's and don'ts to keep in mind:

Do's

DO have goals.

DO volunteer for short events if you want to meet lots of people.

DO volunteer for a committee if you want to build relationships.

DO respect what you need as an introvert.

DO practice your communication skills.

Don'ts

DON'T take on more than you can handle.

3 Keys to Remember

KEY 1: Be open to meeting new people.

KEY 2: Pick your projects with intention.

KEY 3: Keep track of the people you meet.

Chapter 14: Emergencies

Charles was never so glad to get back in his car. He'd scooted out of the association luncheon just as quickly as he could. He didn't know what happened. He was never great at these things, but he'd overcome his old anxiety long ago. Until today. He'd walked up to two people who were chatting, said hello and then just stood there. One never even noticed he was there. The other glanced at him once in surprise, looked confused, and returned to the previous conversation. He then realized they were engaged in a very serious personal conversation but somehow he had missed the cues. He just stood there, feeling humiliated. He extracted himself by pretending something caught his eye and wandered off. After studying a table of flyers for what felt like forever, he glanced at his watchless wrist, feigned surprise at the time and dashed off. Now, sitting in his car, he felt sick. He'd missed the lunch, and on top of his sleepless night, recent bad news and pressing deadlines at work, it was all too much. He felt all his hard work on his networking skills had been for nothing.

Angie's head was spinning. She was sitting at her desk, trying to absorb the conversation she'd just had with her boss. She'd been bugging him forever to let her make a presentation on her project to the executive, then today, bang, just like that, there was an empty slot on tomorrow morning's agenda at the quarterly management conference, and would she like to take the 15 minutes to do her thing? As she sat there sputtering, her boss had said, "I'll take that as a yes. Off you go! It's what you wanted, so now you'd better be ready!" She'd blissfully imagined she'd get a week or so's notice before having to present, if it ever happened, and here it was. Of course, she'd had the presentation ready for weeks, but mentally? It was suddenly here, and she couldn't picture being ready in the morning. She felt a sense of panic and closed her eyes. And all she could see were 200 eyes staring back at her.

What is an introvert's conversation skills emergency?

Good question.

And it's one that you get to answer for yourself.

Broadly speaking, it's anything that might throw you off your game.

Moments like what Charles and Angie were having definitely qualify.

Let's use these predicaments as a lens towards what to do if you have an 'emergency'.

The Networking Blunder - Exercise

Why do you think Charles was so upset?

What caused Charles to make his blunder?

Why do you think Charles was thrown so far off his game when he had been doing so well networking?

What advice would you offer Charles now?

What advice would you offer Charles a week from now, when he has had a bit more time to reflect?

The Looming Presentation - Exercise

Why do you think Angie is so panicked?

What questions would you ask Angie if you had the opportunity?

What advice would you offer Angie now?

What advice would you offer Angie a week from now, after she has made her presentation and has had time to reflect?

Handling Emergencies – The 5 R's

There is no formula for how to handle what feels like an emergency to you.

In the big scheme of things, no one died, and you will survive, but beyond that, how do you get yourself through these moments?

Here are a few strategies to guide you:

Retreat

If you haven't done so already, and you feel the need to, it's ok to retreat, to get a bit of distance from the situation and from other people. Take a break, take a few breaths, drink a glass of water, scribble some notes–do whatever you need to do to calm down.

Reach Out

Reach out to a friend, co-worker or networking buddy for a little advice. Alternatively, get out your journal and write out what happened and see if you can get perspective.

Reflect

Reflect on what happened, or is still happening, from a broader perspective. What have you learned? What could you have done differently? What opportunities for learning and growth do you have?

Rest

In most cases, stepping away from the situation and getting a good night's sleep can do wonders.

Rebound

Once you have calmed yourself down, and have a clear idea of what's going on, brainstorm a plan to get you back on your game. This might include self-care, such as getting some exercise, or rolling up your sleeves to rewrite your proposal.

Remember the 5R's for Emergencies: Retreat ➔ Reach Out ➔ Reflect ➔ Rest ➔ Rebound

Now, let's return to Charles and Angie.

The Networking Blunder - Possibilities

Why do you think Charles was so upset?

> • Charles is in crisis. He was depleted, made a blunder, wasn't able to respond as deftly as usual and was left speechless. He felt humiliated, even though the situation may not have been as bad as he imagined. Now, with his ego was bruised and still feeling embarrassed, his self-confidence has escaped him.

What caused Charles to make his blunder?

> • Charles had gone to an event when he was not at his best (lack of sleep, bad news, work stresses), so he was already vulnerable. This caused him to miss non-verbal cues when he blundered into a private conversation.

Why do you think Charles was thrown so far off his game when he had been doing so well networking?

> • Under different circumstances, Charles would have apologized, shaken it off and moved on. But, because he

wasn't grounded, he allowed the miss to throw him completely off his game.

What advice would you offer Charles now?

- Take a break, don't worry about it, get some rest and deal with your personal matters.

What advice would you offer Charles a week from now, when he has had a bit more time to reflect?

- Ask what he has learned, then reassure him that this was a blip, and he has not lost his networking abilities. To the contrary, he has survived a blunder and is now on the other side of it. Suggest he plan to get out to another event soon, but make it a particularly safe one, and be well rested when he arrives.

The Looming Presentation - Possibilities

Why do you think Angie is so panicked?

- Angie let herself imagine that she would have lots of notice to make her presentation and was surprised. She is experiencing a combination of excitement and nervousness to the degree that it has--momentarily– stopped her dead in her tracks.

What questions would ask Angie if you had the opportunity?

- Is your presentation ready? (Yes). What's the worst that can happen? (She might trip over a few words). Is this a friendly audience? (Yes, she knows them well).

What advice would you offer Angie now?

- Breathe. Get up and move to change the energy. Express your nervousness if need be, then get down to business. You've got this. Pour some tea and walk through your presentation while picturing this particular audience. Tomorrow, get your butterflies to fly in formation.

Remember to find a few smiling faces and talk directly to them.

What advice would you offer Angie a week from now, after she has made her presentation and has had time to reflect?

- Ask her what she learned from the experience, and what she would do differently next time. She probably doesn't need advice, as her answers are within.

As we wrap up this chapter, here are a few helpful caveats to keep in mind:

- If you find yourself in crisis, do whatever you need to do to take care of yourself in the moment.
- Breathe.
- Remember, this is a moment in time. You will get through it.
- Jot some notes to yourself that you can tuck away in your wallet to bring out and read if you get panicked (yes, we're talking about hiding in a bathroom stall, if needed).
- Refer back to Chapter 3: Social Anxiety for additional tips.
- Pay special attention to Chapter 16: Self-Care for Introverts.

What do you think? Have you ever experienced an 'emergency' like the ones described in this chapter? Do you now have things you know you could do to help you cope?

Case Studies

- Although Rebecca was growing by leaps and bounds in terms of sharing her ideas, there were a couple of points where she got totally overwhelmed with not being heard. She could no longer sit quietly on the sidelines! Each time, she learned to take some quiet time out to herself.
- Larry made a rather unfortunate blunder at a networking meeting, just when his confidence had been growing, but he

didn't let it throw him off. Although embarrassed, he took stock and figured out what he needed to do to set things right. A phone call and an apology did the trick.

- Chris' biggest success came from her new ability to quell panic attacks before they started.

- Kelly's emergency came in the form of being asked to make a conference presentation on very short notice. To ensure his message landed, he thought about the different types of people in the audience and structured his words and handouts so that he would have something for everyone.

The Introvert's Survival Guide to Triumphing over Social Emergencies

We all have challenges in life, and blips along the road of wherever we are headed. When things go wrong, simply STOP, take time out and take care of yourself before you carry on.

Here are few do's and don'ts to keep in mind:

Do's

DO trust that you will survive.

DO listen to your gut.

DO tell yourself that you will be ok.

DO appreciate how far you have come.

Don'ts

DON'T beat yourself up.

DON'T panic any more than you are already.

DON'T expect more of yourself at the moment.

DON'T give up.

3 Keys to Remember

KEY 1: Retreat ➔ Reach Out ➔ Reflect ➔ Rest ➔ Rebound

KEY 2: Breathe.

KEY 3: Celebrate your victories.

Chapter 15: Written Communications

"Many introverts naturally see the world in terms of story and symbol. And when we use writing as a tool, we're able to connect the dots and lay out the patterns we see for others."

Lauren Sapala

As an introvert, writing is probably quite natural for you. By intentionally honing your writing skills and applying them to situations where you connect the dots for others, you will contribute even more to the world around you.

While our focus in this book has been on conversation skills, written communications are an important part of interacting with others.

Depending on your work, studies and interests, you may have a lot of written communications in your life or perhaps you just need to manage your email.

Either way, a few written communication fundamentals are worth your attention.

Write to Contribute

Here are just a few ways you can use your written communications to your advantage:

- Offer to summarize what was discussed in meetings.
- Offer to prepare the agenda for meetings you attend.
- Offer to draft reports and presentations for your team.

Write to Contribute - Exercise

The above suggestions have the potential to benefit you, other introverts in our organization, your team members and the company. Can you see how?

As we wrap up this chapter, here are a few helpful caveats to keep in mind:

- If you'd like to improve your written communication skills, there are many resources available to help you. Chances are, though, you are pretty good already.

What do you think? How are your written communication skills? Do they leave a lot to be desired, or do they just need a bit of attention? This is a good one to ask others about, so you can get some feedback.

Case Studies

- Written communications had always been a strength for Rebecca. She found that by applying the written communication tips to what she now understood about adapting to type, she got greater results from her emails.
- Larry began thinking more about his audience, and that most people weren't as analytical as he was, which allowed him to write emails and reports that were less dense.
- Always articulate, Chris learned to write as confidently as she now spoke.

- Kelly had the written communications nailed pretty much already.

The Introvert's Survival Guide to E-Mail

You have the upper hand when it comes to email as you probably are a pretty good writer.

Here are a few do's and don'ts to keep in mind:

Do's

DO use bullet points.

DO model good written communication skills.

DO offer to summarize the meeting by email.

DO offer to send out the next meeting's agenda.

Don'ts

DON'T email when you are angry.

DON'T hide behind email.

3 Keys to Remember

KEY 1: Drafting team emails means they get your stamp.

KEY 2: Keep it brief.

KEY 3: Use bullet points.

Chapter 16: Self-Care for Introverts

"Solitude is for me a fount of healing which makes my life worth living."

C. G. Jung

Self-Care – 4 Essentials

In a nutshell, as an introvert, you need FOUR THINGS to survive and thrive:

1. Time alone daily.

2. Privacy.

3. Quiet zones.

4. Time to reflect.

It's a pretty short list.

These are the core.

Remove any one of these from your life and you will find your energy drained. You won't shrivel up and die, but you might feel like it.

How you make these happen is up to you, of course.

Other Possibilities

You may find there are other things you can do as part of your self-care plan.

Here are a few ideas:

- Learn to say NO.
- Go for a walk at work.
- Bow out from the lunch crowd.
- Put headphones on–even if you have nothing playing.
- Sitting alone in your car may be boring, but you are still alone. It counts.
- Find a quiet area in your workplace where you can get away to think. Borrow an empty office, book a meeting room, sit in the lunchroom when it's empty. Get creative.
- Look for places in your community where you can be 'alone'. Going out for a coffee isn't really time alone, and it won't be quiet, but if you can get yourself in the right headspace, it can be a pretty good alternative.
- Hang out at the library, even if you aren't there to pick up books.

Your Personal Self-Care Plan – Exercise

Pour yourself a cup of tea (or your beverage of choice) and start a fresh page in your notebook.

Jot your ideas in response to the following questions:

- Do I get enough time alone?
- What are some ways in which I can create more time alone in my life?

- Whose support do I need to accomplish this goal?
- What are some ways I can get short bits of time alone during my day, especially if I find an urgent need for it?
- What else do I need to incorporate into my Self-Care Plan (think about quiet time, time to reflect, privacy)?
- Feel free to follow wherever your mind and heart want to go. It's YOUR plan--make it work for you!

As we wrap up this chapter, here are a few helpful caveats to keep in mind:

- Learn to value what makes you tick as an introvert and carve out time to do what you need to do to take care of yourself. If that means you need half an hour of silence to restore your energy while your extrovert co-workers are at the bar, that's fine.
- Do an internet search for "Self-Care for Introverts" – you'll find some great resources.
- Follow a few Twitter, Instagram and Facebook accounts with a focus on introverts.
- Review Chapter 4: Social Anxiety and remind yourself about getting your butterflies to fly in formation.

What do you think? Do you have well-honed instincts for taking care of yourself? Do you honor what your introvert self needs? Are any of the ideas in this chapter new to you? If so, try them out. Keep the ones that make the biggest difference.

Case Studies

- Rebecca took solace in, and gathered energy from, her daily routine of time alone to recharge her batteries.
- Larry used his newly found skills to drum up a broader personal support network for himself.
- Chris was relieved to learn that the things she did naturally to take care of herself were normal and perfectly acceptable.

- Kelly learned how to give his introverted friends time to think and recharge their batteries.

The Introvert's Survival Guide to Self-Care

Self-care that nurtures you as an introvert is essential to your life. It is not a luxury.

Here are a few do's and don'ts to keep in mind:

Do's

DO make time alone a priority.

DO learn to say NO.

DO create quiet zones is your day and life.

DO guard your privacy.

DO speak up if you need time to reflect on a question.

DO adapt your work environment to work for you.

Don'ts

DON'T put time alone on the back burner.

DON'T take care of an extrovert's need for company over time for yourself.

DON'T beat yourself up if you don't want to be with other people.

DON'T just put up with a workplace that is not introvert friendly.

3 Keys to Remember

KEY 1: Take time to be alone.

KEY 2: Make time to collect your thoughts.

KEY 3: Keep your Personal Self-Care Plan handy!

Conclusion

Thanks for making it through to the end of *Conversation Skills: Secrets for Introverts on How to Analyze People, Handle Small Talk with Confidence, Overcome Social Anxiety and Other Highly Effective Communication Tips when Networking with People*. I hope you have found it to be both informative and practical.

Let's conclude by checking in with our four case study subjects:

- Rebecca is feeling heard and is more confident sharing ideas at work. She also feels less anxious about meeting strangers and is enjoying conversations with new people. Rebecca's secret edge is the time she plans alone each day to restore her energy.

- Larry has made great strides in his goal of improving his networking skills. The results are already showing up in his job performance, and he is more relaxed. Larry's secret edge is the genuine curiosity he has developed about the people he meets.

- Chris has achieved her goal of being less stressed at work. She is actively sharing her ideas, has a better relationship with her boss, and is no longer paralyzed if she attends a business event. Chris's secret edge is picking the person she wants to talk to, rather than waiting to be approached.

- Kelly has definitely met his goal of understanding what makes introverts tick. He has also become a better listener. Kelly's secret edge is now having a goal for every interaction.

I hope that learning alongside Rebecca, Larry, Chris and Kelly helped you with applying the skills in this book to your own life and building your confidence.

Your next step is to put the skills into action by thinking about your communications, trying out new approaches when meeting people or sharing your ideas, and learning from both your stumbles and successes. Good luck!

Finally, if you found this book valuable, a review on Amazon is always appreciated!

Made in United States
Troutdale, OR
12/02/2023